SpringerBriefs in Law

More information about this series at http://www.springer.com/series/10164

Marina Foltea

Brexit and the Control of Tobacco Illicit Trade

Marina Foltea
Institute of Law Studies
Polish Academy of Sciences
Warsaw, Poland

ISSN 2192-855X ISSN 2192-8568 (electronic)
SpringerBriefs in Law
ISBN 978-3-030-45978-9 ISBN 978-3-030-45979-6 (eBook)
https://doi.org/10.1007/978-3-030-45979-6

© The Editor(s) (if applicable) and The Author(s) 2020. This book is an open access publication.
Open Access This book is licensed under the terms of the Creative Commons Attribution 4.0 International License (http://creativecommons.org/licenses/by/4.0/), which permits use, sharing, adaptation, distribution and reproduction in any medium or format, as long as you give appropriate credit to the original author(s) and the source, provide a link to the Creative Commons license and indicate if changes were made.
The images or other third party material in this book are included in the book's Creative Commons license, unless indicated otherwise in a credit line to the material. If material is not included in the book's Creative Commons license and your intended use is not permitted by statutory regulation or exceeds the permitted use, you will need to obtain permission directly from the copyright holder.
The use of general descriptive names, registered names, trademarks, service marks, etc. in this publication does not imply, even in the absence of a specific statement, that such names are exempt from the relevant protective laws and regulations and therefore free for general use.
The publisher, the authors and the editors are safe to assume that the advice and information in this book are believed to be true and accurate at the date of publication. Neither the publisher nor the authors or the editors give a warranty, expressed or implied, with respect to the material contained herein or for any errors or omissions that may have been made. The publisher remains neutral with regard to jurisdictional claims in published maps and institutional affiliations.

This Springer imprint is published by the registered company Springer Nature Switzerland AG
The registered company address is: Gewerbestrasse 11, 6330 Cham, Switzerland

Preface

Illicit trade in tobacco products is a global problem, and addressing it requires concerted solutions at the international and regional levels. The EU and its Member States play a significant role in finding adequate solution, at least for its market which loses about 10 billion euro annually from this phenomenon alone. The smuggling of tobacco products also undermines public health policies by making especially cigarettes available in an uncontrolled sales environment and at a substantial discount compared to legal sales channels. Illicit trade in tobacco products is a main source of revenue for organised crime, and it has in some cases been linked to terrorist groups.

The withdrawal of the UK from the EU will undoubtedly change the relations between the two entities on this as well as many issues of vital importance. Against this background, this book discusses how the control of illicit trade in tobacco may change following the process of Brexit focusing mostly on the UK market. Estimating the possible impact of Brexit on illicit trade in tobacco products is a challenging task. Based, however, on the available data and applicable legislation, this book anticipates the problems and provides some policy guidance.

Aside from providing valuable data and insights into tobacco illicit trade market in the UK (and the EU where applicable), this book offers a comprehensive overview of the Brexit process setting the stage for the relevant discussion (Chap. 2). This is followed by providing important available data on the UK tobacco illicit trade market (Chap. 3) and the applicable legal instruments to the issue of control of illicit trade in tobacco (Chaps. 4 and 5). In addition, a number of EU (and occasionally global) anti-illicit trade initiatives are thoroughly discussed (Chap. 6) in order to provide a better sense of direction in the future UK policy on this matter (Chap. 7).

Special thanks for inspiration and support on this research go to my friends Pietro Poretti, Abrie du Plessis and Bryan Khan. The present book is published following research conducted for a study funded by PMI Impact, a grant award initiative of Philip Morris International ("PMI"). In the performance of its research, the author maintained full independence from PMI. The views and opinions expressed in this document are those of Grantee and do not necessarily reflect the views of PMI. Responsibility for the information and views expressed in this study lies entirely with the author. Neither PMI, nor any of its affiliates, nor person acting on their behalf may be held responsible for any use which may be made of the information contained herein.

Warsaw, Poland					Marina Foltea
March 2020

Contents

1	**Introduction**	1
	References	3
2	**The UK Process of Leaving the EU**	5
	2.1 State of Play and Possible Brexit Scenarios	5
	2.2 Relevant Brexit Instruments	8
	2.2.1 The Withdrawal Agreement	8
	2.2.2 The Political Declaration	9
	2.3 Possible Impact of Brexit on the Control of Illicit Trade in Tobacco	10
	2.3.1 Impact on the UK Legislation	11
	2.3.2 Impact on Trade in Goods and Customs Controls	12
	2.4 Territorial Impact	14
	2.4.1 The Irish Border	15
	2.4.2 Gibraltar	16
	References	18
3	**The Issue of Illicit Tobacco Trade in the UK**	21
	3.1 Definition and Forms of Illicit Trade	22
	3.2 The Duty-Free Regime (Personal Allowances)	23
	3.3 UK Illicit Tobacco Trade Data	24
	3.3.1 UK Government Information	24
	3.3.2 Tobacco Industry Information	25
	3.3.3 Comparison with EU-Wide Data	28
	References	29
4	**UK Relevant Legal and Enforcement Frameworks**	33
	4.1 Relevant Legal Framework	34
	4.1.1 Fiscal Measures	34
	4.1.2 Import Duties	40
	4.1.3 Tobacco Regulations	43

	4.2	The Enforcement Framework	46
		4.2.1 UK Institutions	47
		4.2.2 Current Collaboration with EU Agencies and Bodies	48
		4.2.3 Possible Forms of Post-Brexit Cooperation with EU Agencies	51
	References		55
5	**EU and Member States Agreements with the Tobacco Industry**		61
	5.1	Voluntary Memoranda of Understanding	61
	5.2	Binding Agreements	63
	References		65
6	**Key EU and Global Anti-illicit Trade Initiatives**		67
	6.1	2014 EU Tobacco Products Directive (TPD-2)	67
	6.2	WHO FCTC Protocol to Eliminate Illicit Trade in Tobacco Products (ITP)	72
	References		76
7	**Conclusions and Recommendations**		79

Abbreviations

2018 Withdrawal Act	The European Union (Withdrawal) Act 2018
2019 Political Declaration	Political Declaration setting out the framework for the future relationship between the European Union and the UK, 19 October 2019
2019 Withdrawal Agreement	Agreement on the withdrawal of the UK of Great Britain and Northern Ireland from the European Union and the European Atomic Energy Community, 19 October 2019
BAT	British American Tobacco
CCWP	Customs Cooperation Working Party of the European Council
CETA	EU-Canada Comprehensive Economic and Trade Agreement
DExEU	Department for Exiting the European Union
ECJ	European Court of Justice
EEA	European Economic Area
EFTA	European Free Trade Association
EMCS	Excise Movement and Control System
EMPACT	European Multidisciplinary Platform against Criminal Threats
EU	European Union
EUIPO	European Union Intellectual Property Office
FCLOs	Fiscal Crime Liaison Officers
FTA(s)	Free trade agreement(s)
HMC&E	Her Majesty's Customs and Excise
HMRC	Her Majesty's Revenue and Customs
HRT	Hand-rolling tobacco
APPG	Illicit Trade All Party Parliamentary Group
ITP	Protocol to Eliminate Illicit Trade in Tobacco Products

JTI	Japan Tobacco International
MET	Minimum Excise Tax
MILs	Minimum Indicative Limits
MOP	Meeting of the Parties
MoU	Memorandum of Understanding
MPs	Members of Parliament
NAO	National Audit Office
NCA	National Crime Agency
OECD	Organisation for Economic Co-operation and Development
OJ	Official Journal of the European Union
OLAF	European Anti-Fraud Office
PM	Prime Minister
PMI	Philip Morris International
RUSI	Royal United Services Institute
TEU	Treaty on European Union
TMA	Tobacco Manufacturers Association
TPD-2	Tobacco Product Directive 2014/40/EU
TTB	Total tax burden
UK	United Kingdom
UKIPO	Intellectual Property Office of the United Kingdom
VAT	Value-added tax
WCO	World Customs Organisation
WHO	World Health Organisation
FCTC	WHO Framework Convention on Tobacco Control
WTO	World Trade Organisation

List of Tables

Table 4.1   Tobacco products duty rates.   36
Table 4.2   Import tariffs on tobacco products from third countries   41

Chapter 1
Introduction

Over three and a half years after the popular vote, Brexit remains a moving target, particularly with regard to the future relationship between the EU and the UK. The content of this subproject, whilst it was up to date at the time of writing, may have been superseded by recent events.

Estimating the impact of Brexit on *licit* trade is a challenging task. Over three and a half years after the referendum, many aspects of the separation between the European Union (EU) and the United Kingdom (UK) remain undefined. Assessing the impact of Brexit on *illicit* trade, by definition a covert and constantly evolving activity, is even more difficult. Although not a priority in the Brexit discussions, the issue of illicit trade in tobacco products has nevertheless attracted some attention, mainly in relation to the border between Ireland and Northern Ireland, recalling past instances of smuggling activities alongside the UK-Irish border. Limited references to illicit tobacco trade are contained in the *Agreement on the withdrawal of the United Kingdom of Great Britain and Northern Ireland from the European Union and the European Atomic Energy Community of 19 October 2019* (2019 Withdrawal Agreement) with regard to Gibraltar and Spain.

The UK Government's commitment to fight illicit tobacco trade has remained strong since the publication of its first comprehensive strategy in 2000,[1] irrespective of the political leadership. Over the years, the estimated market share of illicit tobacco products has diminished, most notably for cigarettes. While approximately 1 in 5 cigarettes smoked in the UK in the year 2000 were smuggled, recent estimates suggest that the current ratio is down to 1 in 10. It is assumed that Brexit will not affect Government resolve to continue the fight against illicit tobacco trade in the UK and more widely in the EU.

Brexit will most definitely modify the relationship between the UK and the EU. The EU is both a single market and a customs union. As an EU member, the UK had the highest possible level of integration with other EU countries. Several post-Brexit scenarios have been envisaged following the immediate aftermath of the 2016 referendum. The four more recurrent scenarios are (i) *'Soft Brexit'*—UK remains in

---

[1] HM Customs and Excise and HM Treasury (2000)—Tackling tobacco smuggling.

the EU's single market, but not in its customs union; (ii) *Theresa May's 2018 Deal*—UK leaves the single market, but maintains a customs union with the EU; (iii) *Boris Johnson's 2019 Deal*—UK leaves the single market and the customs union, and concludes a free trade agreement with the EU similar to the EU-Canada agreement; or (iv) *'Hard Brexit'*—future UK-EU relations are simply based on World Trade Organization (WTO) terms.

The terminology such as 'soft-' and 'hard-Brexit' has not always been used consistently. The four mentioned scenarios are used however to weigh the economic pros and cons of Brexit, e.g. on British exports (goods and services) to the EU, and on the UK's attractiveness as a destination for foreign direct investment.[2] These four scenarios have been retained for the purpose of this book as well. Their pertinence may somewhat be limited by the fact that illicit trade is, by definition, an unregulated activity. The different scenarios will however help capture the varying degrees of flexibility for post-Brexit UK that may have an impact on illicit tobacco trade as well as on other matters.

For instance, one could argue that the scenario that offers the lowest possible level of integration, i.e., 'hard Brexit', has the highest potential to disrupt illicit trade, including in tobacco products, due to the introduction of tighter border controls compared to the EU frictionless borders. But, the UK is a target country for illicit tobacco with no significant domestic manufacturing. Thus, increased checks at the border may help keep illicit products out of the national market, leading to more seizures and generally deterring illicit imports. Whether the UK will manage to efficiently control tobacco illicit trade into its territory will also depend on the UK's readiness to cope with post-Brexit realities. Sufficient resources need to be allocated to border control both for merchandise traffic and immigration. In addition, the disruption of existing cooperation between the EU and the UK in terms of information exchange, investigations, and enforcement operations outside of the national territory, could seriously undermine the UK's capability to fight illicit trade. This will have to be duly factored in by the post-Brexit UK governments.

Against this background, this book assesses the consequences of Brexit for illicit trade in tobacco products in the UK. Based on the currently applicable legal framework, it looks at the significance of a possible non-application of the *acquis communautaire* in the UK in matters relating to tobacco anti-illicit trade legislation, and analyses several avenues for possible future cooperation between the UK and the EU in this area, as well as possible regulatory scenarios and their consequences.

The book comprises six main sections. After the introduction (in this chapter), Chap. 2 discusses the state of play of Brexit and possible outcomes for the invocation of the Article 50 of the Treaty of European Union procedure. Chapter 3 illustrates the data and trends of illicit tobacco trade in the UK. Chapter 4 describes the relevant legal (e.g. trade and fiscal measures) and enforcement frameworks in the UK on this matter and suggests possible post-Brexit scenarios for sustainably tackling the control of tobacco illicit trade. Chapter 5 focuses on the relevance of pre-existing

---

[2]London School of Economics Blog (2019)—Brexit will leave the UK worse off economically in all scenarios.

arrangements between the EU and/or its Member States and the tobacco industry in the control of illicit trade in Europe more widely and the options the UK has with respect to these agreements. Chapter 6 then analyses the relevance of key EU and global anti-illicit trade initiatives which can be inspirational for the UK in building its post-Brexit policy on this matter. Finally, and drawing from the analyses in the book, Chap. 7 offers some recommendations and conclusions on what measures are of interest to the UK in controlling illicit trade in tobacco as an EU outsider.

References

HM Customs and Excise and HM Treasury (2000) Tackling tobacco smuggling. The Stationery Office, London

London School of Economics Blog (2019) Brexit will leave the UK worse off economically in all scenarios, 30 Nov 2019. https://blogs.lse.ac.uk/businessreview/2019/11/30/brexit-will-leave-the-uk-worse-off-economically-in-all-scenarios. Accessed 24 Feb 2020

Open Access This chapter is licensed under the terms of the Creative Commons Attribution 4.0 International License (http://creativecommons.org/licenses/by/4.0/), which permits use, sharing, adaptation, distribution and reproduction in any medium or format, as long as you give appropriate credit to the original author(s) and the source, provide a link to the Creative Commons license and indicate if changes were made.

The images or other third party material in this chapter are included in the chapter's Creative Commons license, unless indicated otherwise in a credit line to the material. If material is not included in the chapter's Creative Commons license and your intended use is not permitted by statutory regulation or exceeds the permitted use, you will need to obtain permission directly from the copyright holder.

Chapter 2
The UK Process of Leaving the EU

On 23 June 2016, people in the UK and in Gibraltar cast their vote on the *United Kingdom European Union Membership Referendum*, also known as the *EU Referendum* or the *Brexit Referendum*. Asked to decide whether the country should remain a member of, or leave the European Union, 51.89% of those who took part in the vote chose to leave. Although legally the referendum was non-binding, the UK government of that time, led by Prime Minister David Cameron, had promised to implement the result. The official EU withdrawal process, commonly known as '*Brexit*' was initiated on 29 March 2017. The complex process is based on the never before used Article 50 of the *Treaty on the European Union* (TEU). Brexit was originally due to happen on 29 March 2019, i.e. two years after then Prime Minister May triggered the formal process to leave and kicked off negotiations with the European Union.

2.1 State of Play and Possible Brexit Scenarios

The popular vote neither settled the debate nor clarified the tangled question of what should come next. So far, the process of withdrawal has been marked by intense political debate, ministerial resignations, and much speculation. Prime Minister May's resignation announced on 24 May 2019 and the ensuing leadership contest slowed down the domestic decision-making process. Discussions, at home and with Brussels resumed with the arrival of Boris Johnson, a pro-Brexit leader, at 10 Downing Street on 24 July 2019. Three and a half years after the Brexit vote, the last word has not yet been spoken regarding the terms of this unprecedented divorce. The impact of Brexit on economic activities, both licit and illicit, including trade in tobacco products, therefore remains hard to predict.

Although TEU Art. 50 stating "*Any Member State may decide to withdraw from the Union in accordance with its own constitutional requirements*" has never been triggered before, some relevant precedents exist for all scenarios considered.[1] Under

---

[1] Consolidated version of the Treaty on European Union, OJ C 326, 26.10.2012.

the first scenario, i.e. '*soft Brexit*', the UK remains in the EU's single market, but not its customs union. The *European Economic Area (EEA) Agreement* that brings together the EU Member States and the three EEA EFTA States—Iceland, Liechtenstein and Norway—is an example of how such relationship could be structured.[2] The second scenario consists of the deal negotiated by the former Prime Minister (PM) May where the UK leaves the single market, but maintains a customs union with the EU. In this case, the arrangement between the EU and Turkey presents an interesting precedent.[3] Under the third scenario, which reflects the most recent arrangement negotiated with the EU by the current PM Boris Johnson and announced in October 2019, the UK leaves the single market and the customs union and agrees to a comprehensive free trade agreement with the EU. The precedents in these case are practically all the existing FTAs globally. Finally, the fourth and last scenario foresees a '*hard Brexit*', i.e. a situation where absent any comprehensive agreement between the parties, future UK–EU relations would be based on World Trade Organization (WTO) terms. This is also common for the countries which are WTO Members but have not concluded additional FTAs among themselves.

Disagreements in the House of Commons regarding the arrangement negotiated with the EU by the current PM Boris Johnson resulted in arranging a short notice general election, held on 12 December 2019. Not surprisingly, the then ongoing process of leaving the EU topped the list of the electorate's concerns in the run up to the election. The Conservatives campaigned to get Brexit done by pushing through Johnson's deal and thus structure future economic relations with the EU on the basis of a trade agreement. Labour on the other hand, promised a new arrangement with the EU followed by a popular vote, whereas the Liberal Democrats pledged to fight for a second referendum with the option to stay in the EU unless they win a majority and can enact their policy of revoking TEU Article 50. Many did not hesitate to call the elections "historic", with voters facing a "historic choice".[4] Quite historic was also the landslide victory of the Conservative Party, which received an eighty seat majority (their largest majority since 1987) and winning 43.6% of the vote (the highest percentage by any party since 1979).

The election finally brought clarity to the Brexit process. Thanks to a sizeable majority of the Conservative Party in the UK Parliament, the latter accepted Johnson's deal on 23 January 2020. The UK Government issued and deposited Britain's instrument of ratification of the 2019 Withdrawal Agreement on 29 January 2020. The Agreement was ratified by the Council of the European Union on 30 January 2020, following the consent of the European Parliament on 29 January 2020. The United Kingdom's withdrawal from the European Union took effect on 11 p.m.

---

[2] The EEA Agreement was signed in Porto on 2 May 1992 and entered into force on 1 January 1994. Liechtenstein joined on 1 May 1995. See EFTA (2020) and UK in a Changing Europe (2019) EU-Turkey Customs Union.

[3] The EU-Turkey Customs Union was established on 1 January 1996 by Decision No 1/95 of the EC-Turkey Association Council. See EC-Turkey Association Council (1995), and UK in a Changing Europe (2018).

[4] Brown (2019).

2.1 State of Play and Possible Brexit Scenarios

GMT on 31 January 2020, and at that moment the Withdrawal Agreement entered into force, as per its Art. 185.

Pursuant to Art. 126, the 2019 Withdrawal Agreement provides for a transition period until at least 31 December 2020, during which the UK remains in the single market, in order to ensure frictionless trade until a long-term relationship is agreed. The transition period can be extended once for up to one or two years by a EU–UK Joint Committee, as long as it decides to do so before 1 July 2020.[5]

During the transition, all EU legislation, rules and court decisions will continue to apply to and in the UK as if it were a Member State.[6] This means the UK will continue to participate in the EU customs union and the single market (with all four freedoms) and in all Union policies. Any changes to EU legislation or rules will automatically apply to the UK.

After the entry into force of the 2019 Withdrawal Agreement, the attention shifted to the future EU–UK relationship, and in particular to the announced trade deal. The EU-Canada Comprehensive Economic and Trade Agreement (CETA) entered into force provisionally on 21 September 2017 has often been cited as a basis for a future relationship.[7] The non-binding Political Declaration on the future EU–UK relationship, closely connected to the 2019 Withdrawal Agreement—the two Brexit texts negotiated so far by the parties (described in Sect. 2.2 below)—suggests that a free trade agreement could be at the core of the future relationship between the UK and the EU.[8]

However, there is only a limited amount of time for a process that is expected to be difficult and tense. For instance, it took Canada and the EU seven years to negotiate CETA. A crucial point will be how much the UK will wish to diverge from existing EU rules. On this aspect, despite the centrality of Brexit in the December 2019 elections, the campaign had little to say about how the UK would approach the future relationship with the EU. While the UK Government has argued that a trade deal can be concluded by the end of December 2020, European leaders have repeatedly sounded alarm bells, warning that the UK's imposed deadline leaves little time, and that achieving a comprehensive trade deal in 11 months is unrealistic.[9] As of February 2020, the latter remains subject of negotiations yet to come. Talks are set to commence on 3 March. Should the parties not manage to reach an agreement by the end of 2020 and the transition period is not extended, a no-deal (or 'cliff-edge') Brexit would be the default outcome in 2021.

---

[5] Art. 132 'Extension of the transition period', 2019 Withdrawal Agreement.
[6] Art. 127 'Scope of the Transition', 2019 Withdrawal Agreement.
[7] See O'Carroll (2019) Can UK get 'super Canada-plus' trade deal with EU by end of 2020?
[8] Para. 3 of the 2019 Political Declaration reads "[…] *this declaration establishes the parameters of an ambitious, broad, deep and flexible partnership across trade and economic cooperation with a comprehensive and balanced Free Trade Agreement at its core, law enforcement and criminal justice, foreign policy, security and defence and wider areas of cooperation.*"
[9] Euronews (2020) Post-Brexit Guide: Where are we now—and how did we get here?

2.2 Relevant Brexit Instruments

The future relationship between the UK and the EU remains to be designed. Negotiations have so far delivered two tangible instruments: a Withdrawal Agreement and a non-binding Political Declaration. For the issue of illicit trade in tobacco products, these instruments are of limited relevance with the exception of the special provisions applicable to the overseas territory of Gibraltar and, to a lesser extent, to the Irish border.

2.2.1 The Withdrawal Agreement

After months of intense negotiations, on 14 November 2018 London and Brussels announced that they had agreed on the conditions for Brexit, set out in the Withdrawal Agreement (the '*2018 Withdrawal Agreement*').[10] This text contains the proposed terms on how to implement Brexit and illustrates the general features of the relationship between the two sides in the short to medium term. The *2018 Withdrawal Agreement* has remained in form of a draft; the House of Commons has voted down the text three consecutive times in the first quarter of 2019 during the May Government.[11] After taking office, PM Johnson followed up on his promise to renegotiate the *2018 Withdrawal Agreement* with the EU and surprised many when he rapidly secured an alternative deal from the EU27 in the autumn of 2019.

The 2019 Withdrawal Agreement[12] which entered into force on 31 January 2020 largely mirrors its predecessor. The main differences are in the *Protocol on Ireland/Northern Ireland*—or the '*backstop*' as it is commonly known. The *2019 Withdrawal Agreement* provides how goods shall be treated during the transition period starting on Brexit day (31 January 2020) and ending on 31 December 2020. Like its predecessor, the 2019 Withdrawal Agreement does not offer much detail on how the two sides will interact after Brexit. Quite unsurprisingly, the issue of illicit trade, including tobacco products, did not capture much attention in the negotiations.

The 541-page long 2019 Withdrawal Agreement only uses the word "illicit" in relation to tobacco once, namely in the *Protocol on Gibraltar*, where the UK undertakes to ensure that the ratification of the *WHO Framework Convention on Tobacco Control* (FCTC) and of the *Protocol to Eliminate Illicit Trade in Tobacco Products* (ITP) is extended to Gibraltar by 30 June 2020.[13] The word "smuggling" appears four

---

[10] HM Government (2018) Agreement on the withdrawal of the United Kingdom of Great Britain and Northern Ireland from the European Union and the European Atomic Energy Community, as endorsed by leaders at a special meeting of the European Council on 25 November 2018. See also, European Commission (2019) The EU–UK Withdrawal Agreement explained.

[11] On 15 January 2019 (432 to 202), on 12 March 2019 (391 to 242) and lastly on 29 March 2019 (344 votes to 286).

[12] HM Government (2019) New Withdrawal Agreement and Political Declaration.

[13] 2019 Withdrawal Agreement, Protocol on Gibraltar, Article 3 para 3.

2.2 Relevant Brexit Instruments

times: three times in the *Protocol on Gibraltar* and one in the *Protocol relating to the Sovereign Base Areas of the United Kingdom of Great Britain and Northern Ireland in Cyprus*.[14] Finally, the 2019 Withdrawal Agreement mentions the word "tobacco" six times. Beside the above-mentioned *Protocol on Gibraltar*,[15] "tobacco" is mentioned in Annex 2 and 3 to the *Protocol on Ireland/Northern Ireland* which contains references to the *2014 EU Tobacco Products Directive*[16] and to *Council Directive 2011/64 on the structure and rates of excise duty applied to manufactured tobacco*. These provisions of EU law, discussed in the subsequent sections, will continue to apply to and in the UK in respect of Northern Ireland.

2.2.2 The Political Declaration

Beside the *2019 Withdrawal Agreement*, the UK and the EU agreed on a non-binding statement of future relations in the form of a *Political Declaration Setting out the Framework for the Future Relationship between the European Union and the United Kingdom* (2019 Political Declaration). Like the Withdrawal Agreement, the Political Declaration, was first signed on 25 November 2018 by the Government of former PM Theresa May. The Political Declaration sketches out the kind of long-term relation that the UK and the EU want to have in a range of areas, including trade, defence, and security. By and large, the 2019 Political Declaration reflects the content of the 2018 document. With respect to certain elements however, the new version has been 'watered down', reflecting the different stance of the May and Johnson premierships. In particular, the aspirations for a close future trading arrangement seem somewhat reduced in the new text. For instance, while the original version aspired to an "as close as possible" future trading relationship with the EU, that phrase was replaced by "ambitious" in the revised text. Some commentators have suggested that the current UK Government aims at establishing more distant economic ties with the EU than what its predecessor had in mind, a relationship characterised by less regulatory alignment and greater trade barriers between Britain and its largest trading partner.[17]

Despite the very general language, some elements of the 2019 Political Declaration can nevertheless be retained for the purpose of this work. For instance, document opens with the general statement that *"The future relationship [...] [w]hile it cannot amount to the rights or obligations of membership, [] should be approached with high ambition with regard to its scope and depth, and [...] might evolve over time"*

---

[14] 2019 Withdrawal Agreement, Protocol relating to the Sovereign Base Areas of the United Kingdom of Great Britain and Northern Ireland in Cyprus, Article 2 para 6.

[15] The 2019 Withdrawal Agreement, Protocol on Gibraltar refers to the Memoranda of Understanding concluded between the Kingdom of Spain and the United Kingdom in November 2018 in relation to citizens' rights, tobacco and other products, cooperation on environmental matters and cooperation in police and customs matters, as well as the agreement to conclude a treaty on taxation and the protection of financial interests.

[16] Directive 2014/40/EU of the European Parliament and of the Council of 3 April 2014.

[17] See, for instance Milliken and John (2019).

(Paragraph 5). With regard to tariffs, Paragraph 22 provides that *"The economic partnership should through a Free Trade Agreement ensure no tariffs, fees, charges or quantitative restrictions across all sectors with appropriate and modern accompanying rules of origin, and with ambitious customs arrangements that are in line with the Parties' objectives and principles above."* With regard to customs, *"The Parties will put in place ambitious customs arrangements []. In doing so, the Parties envisage making use of all available facilitative arrangements and technologies [] and ensuring that customs authorities are able to protect the Parties' respective financial interests and enforce public policies. To this end, the [UK and the EU] intend to consider [] administrative cooperation in customs matters and mutual assistance, including [] through the exchange of information to combat customs fraud and other illegal activity []"*, as stated in Paragraph 24.

On global cooperation, Paragraph 75 of the 2019 Political Declaration promotes cooperation in international fora, where there is mutual interest, including in the area of public health and consumer protection. Another aspect of the future relationship relevant to the fight against illicit tobacco trade is law enforcement and judicial cooperation in criminal matters, as discussed in Paragraphs 80–89 of the 2019 Political Declaration. According to Paragraph 82, the future relationship *"will provide for comprehensive, closed, balanced and reciprocal law enforcement and judicial cooperation in criminal matters, with the view to delivering strong operational capabilities for the purposes of the prevention, investigation, detection and prosecution of criminal offences, taking into account the geographic proximity, shared and evolving threats the Parties face, [and] the mutual benefits to the safety and security of their citizens [...]"*. The three main areas of cooperation, to be covered by future arrangements, are data exchange; operational cooperation between law enforcement authorities and judicial cooperation in criminal matters; as well as anti-money laundering and counter terrorism financing.

The press that covered Brexit only made sporadic references to the problem of illicit tobacco trade in relation to departure of the UK from the EU, in particular in relation to the risk of increased smuggling across the Irish border. As mentioned above, the Withdrawal Agreement (both in the original 2018 and revised 2019 versions) mainly refers to illicit trade and tobacco in the Protocol on Gibraltar, an instrument sought by the Spanish Government which is discussed in Sect. 2.4 below. The following sub-section maps out in greater detail the possible impact of Brexit on the control of illicit trade in the region.

2.3 Possible Impact of Brexit on the Control of Illicit Trade in Tobacco

The impact of Brexit on the control of illicit trade in tobacco products can be analysed by looking at how the completion of the TEU Art. 50 procedure may impact UK legislation as well as the regulation of the UK–EU border. As an EU Member, the

UK was bound to EU legislation, including legislation that directly or indirectly relates to tobacco control and trade. The most relevant legislation for this discussion is the UK law (including in the form of EU-derived domestic legislation), and the *EU Withdrawal Act of 2018*,[18] which provides for a retention of the directly applicable EU legislation. Post-Brexit, the UK will be able to amend its legislation unilaterally where and how it deems necessary, as well as to refrain from adopting new rules developed by the EU. This may result in differences in the applicable regulatory frameworks to the relevant territories—a situation that illicit activities can try to exploit. Due to the geographic situation of the UK and the cross-border nature of illicit tobacco trade, two areas of the UK territory are of particular interest from this perspective, namely Gibraltar and the area surrounding the Irish border.

2.3.1 Impact on the UK Legislation

Legal certainty is necessary for economic activity to flourish whereas, typically, illicit activities attempt to benefit from legal uncertainty. Because of the way in which EU law works and how it is implemented at the national level, the withdrawal from the EU would have a major impact on future UK legislation.

EU law today covers a broad range of areas but not all EU legislation has the same effect on Member States. There are two main ways in which EU law applies, namely through regulations or directives. Starting from the latter, once passed at the EU level, directives have to be implemented (or 'transposed') into domestic legislation before they can be binding on individuals and companies.[19] In the UK, directives are implemented either by primary legislation (i.e. an Act of Parliament) or, much more commonly, by secondary legislation (a Statutory Instrument). The implementing legislation is domestic legislation and thus part of the UK's legal system. For instance, in the area of tobacco control, the UK has adopted the *Tobacco Products (Traceability and Security Features) Regulations 2019* to implement track and trace and security features for tobacco in the UK, as required by the *EU Tobacco Products Directive*, discussed in detail below. On the contrary, EU regulations, once passed at the EU level, are directly applicable and binding on individuals and companies in the Member States without the need for national implementation measures. There are currently about 12,000 EU regulations in operation in the UK. The same applies to decisions, although these are only binding on those to whom they are addressed.

From the moment the UK left the EU and once the transition period is completed, EU law will stop flowing into the UK legal system. Today, EU law applies pursuant

---

[18] European Union (Withdrawal) Act 2018.

[19] EU directives may contain minimum and maximum (or full) harmonisation requirements. In the case of minimum harmonisation, a directive sets minimum standards, often in recognition of the fact that the legal systems in some EU countries have already set higher standards. In this case, EU countries have the right to set higher standards than those foreseen in the directive. In the case of maximum harmonisation, EU countries may not introduce rules that are stricter than those set in the directive.

to the *European Communities Act 1972*. Accodring to the 2018 Withdrawal Act UK will not have to consider the EU law as a source of law and will not be bound by the EU institutions previously legislating for the UK. To avoid a situation where the withdrawal would create a legislative black hole from the moment of Brexit (or where there is also a transition period after Brexit) the 2018 Withdrawal Act provides for a retention of most existing directly applicable EU law in UK after the exit day by creating a new body of 'retained EU law'.[20] As for EU-derived domestic legislation (the body of UK legislation resulting from the implementation of EU directives), the 2018 Withdrawal Act foresees that it will preserve the same effect in domestic law as it had immediately before the exit day.[21]

Past Brexit day, the UK would decide whether to mirror any post-exit developments of the EU law into domestic law by amending that body of 'retained EU law'. For instance, should the EU amend the *2014 Tobacco Products Directive* after Brexit, the UK would in principle be free to decide whether to undertake the changes necessary to reflect such amendment in the UK legislation, or not. Similarly, any new or amended EU regulation relevant to the issue of illicit tobacco trade would, as such, not apply in the UK. Should the UK deem specific legislative content (or parts thereof) necessary in the UK, it would have to enact corresponding domestic legislation.

2.3.2 Impact on Trade in Goods and Customs Controls

The EU is the UK's largest trading partner. In 2017, 44% of all UK exports went to the EU, while 53% of all UK imports came from the EU.[22] The possibility of introducing tariff and non-tariff barriers to goods originating in the EU imported into the UK (and vice versa) depends on the type of agreement that the two parties will eventually negotiate. Options have evolved over time and are now reflected in the four Brexit scenarios discussed above, ranging from *'Soft Brexit'* to *'Hard Brexit'*. The pros and cons of each approach have been the subject of intense debates, mainly from the perspective of UK manufacturers and exporters.[23]

The collection of import tariffs on tobacco products from the EU under the different scenarios and the resulting possible price increase or decrease, is discussed below in Sect. 4.1. Beside tariffs, also relevant for the question of illicit trade in tobacco products is the post-Brexit approach to border controls.

Today, goods between the UK and the EU circulate freely, and the UK's management of the border is heavily influenced by the country's (former) EU Membership.

---

[20] Under the heading 'Retention of existing EU law', Section 3 of the 2018 Withdrawal Act states *"Direct EU legislation, so far as operative immediately before exit day, forms part of domestic law on and after exit day."*

[21] Section 2, 2018 Withdrawal Act, *"EU-derived domestic legislation, as it has effect in domestic law immediately before exit day, continues to have effect in domestic law on and after exit day."*

[22] Ward (2019).

[23] See for instance UK Parliament (2017) European Union Committee Brexit: trade in goods, and also UNCTAD (2019) No-deal Brexit: the trade winners and losers.

2.3 Possible Impact of Brexit on the Control of Illicit Trade in Tobacco

Brexit is likely to change this, in particular under the scenarios that foresee structuring EU–UK relations on the basis of a trade agreement (third scenario) or in case of 'Hard Brexit'. Time is of the essence. The UK Government has acknowledged that the possibility of facing a period of "less than optimal" border functioning is concrete.[24] The Government, wherever possible, would have to put in place coping responses for which efficacy remains impossible to predict. While individuals and businesses alike would be negatively impacted by a sub-optimal border to varying degrees, those involved in illicit activities, including illicit tobacco trade, could try to profit.

The UK border is a complex concept. It can be crossed by people or goods coming to or leaving the UK by air, sea or land at more than 270 recognised crossing points.[25] Total imports into the UK in 2017 amounted to a value of £476 billion, comprising £259 billion imports from the EU and £217 billion imports from the rest of the world.[26] New customs controls, tariffs, and non-tariff barriers might apply to trade in both directions.

Changes to the import and export procedures would result in more bureaucracy. Increased red tape is burdensome for economic operators and for customs authorities alike. For instance, in case of 'Hard Brexit', absent any type of arrangement, one can expect that trade under 'third country' status would result in customs declarations and upfront Value Added Tax (VAT) payments. In some cases, firms may need export licenses. In a report published in October 2018, HMRC foresees that the number of customs declarations that the UK authorities need to process might rise from 55 million a year to 260 million.[27] New border systems would be needed and their deployment takes time.

UK ports could be put under accrued stress. Reports by Dover and Kent Councils have warned of possible massive disruptions and the UK Government also foresees disturbances in the Channel ports.[28] Industries relying on 'just-in-time' supplies of parts (e.g. car industry) or fresh products (e.g. food and drink industries) have voiced similar concerns.

Both sides are preparing contingency plans in case of 'Hard Brexit'. In the UK, the Department for Exiting the European Union (DExEU) is responsible for coordinating EU exit-related issues, including those affecting the border. Because of

---

[24] According to the National Audit Office (NAO), *"The government does not have enough time to put in place all of the infrastructure, systems and people required for fully effective border operations on day one. It has decided to prioritise security and flow of traffic over compliance activity in the short term."* National Audit Office (2018) The UK border: preparedness for EU exit, p. 10.

[25] National Audit Office (2017) The UK border: issues and challenges for government's management of the border in light of the UK's planned departure from the EU, p. 8.

[26] In addition, total exports in 2017 amounted to £339 billion, comprising £164 billion exports to the EU and £175 billion exports to the rest of the world. Total EU trade was worth £423 billion and total rest of the world trade was worth £392 billion in 2017. See Office for National Statistics (2018) Pink Book, Table 9.4.

[27] See, for instance O'Carrol (2017).https://www.theguardian.com/politics/2017/mar/31/uk-ports-struggling-fivefold-rise-customs-brexit-hmrc-mps-declaration.

[28] Sandford (2018).

the uncertainty in the outcome of the Brexit negotiations (that has persisted since the creation of the DExEU in July 2016), it remains unclear whether the necessary customs system, resources, and infrastructure will be ready on time. For instance, to fully enforce compliance regimes from day one, HMRC needs infrastructure to track goods, whereas Border Force require space and facilities to physically examine goods. As for the additional human resources, Border Force has estimated that it could require around 2000 staff to meet all requirements in the event of *'Hard Brexit'*, including compliance with WTO rules and other international obligations.[29] New staff requirements needs time for recruitment, security clearance, and training.

The customs system is another critical element. HMRC's implementation of the Customs Declaration Service (CDS) started before the EU Referendum in June 2016, but following the vote and the resulting uncertainty, significant time has been lost. Depending on the final outcome of Brexit implementation, the system might need to be able to handle multiple times the current number of customs declarations each year, and a significantly higher number of traders (estimated between 145,000 and 250,000) may have to make customs declarations for the first time.[30]

2.4 Territorial Impact

The United Kingdom consists of four constituent countries: England, Scotland, Wales, and Northern Ireland. The UK also has fourteen British Overseas Territories, including Gibraltar, and Akrotiri and Dhekelia on the island of Cyprus.[31] The Brexit vote was not unanimous: while voters in England (including Gibraltar) and Wales supported Brexit, Scotland and Northern Ireland favoured to remain in the EU. Beside the island of Great Britain, Northern Ireland (a region located in the north east of the island of Ireland and which is part of the UK) and Gibraltar are of particular relevance to the question of how Brexit may impact illicit trade in tobacco products between the EU and the UK. Both regions share borders with EU Members, namely with the Republic of Ireland (560 km and 1700 crossing points) and Spain.

As a result of a process known as devolution, there are distinct legislatures and governments in Scotland, Wales, and Northern Ireland (devolved governments), which have powers over a range of policy areas which had previously been the preserve of the UK Government. The control of competencies coming back from the EU is contested between the UK and the devolved governments. The lack of rules in the largely unwritten constitution means that there are no clear ways of resolving the resulting conflicts. For instance, the duty system is not a devolved administration issue and

---

[29] See, for instance, Crawford (2018).

[30] National Audit Office (2018) The UK border: preparedness for EU exit, p. 36.

[31] The other twelve overseas territories are Anguilla; Bermuda; the British Antarctic Territory; the British Indian Ocean Territory; the British Virgin Islands; the Cayman Islands; the Falkland Islands; Gibraltar; Montserrat; Saint Helena, Ascension and Tristan da Cunha; the Turks and Caicos Islands; the Pitcairn Islands; South Georgia and the South Sandwich Islands.

therefore no 'devolved administration interests' arise. However, health is a devolved matter and the devolved administrations each have tobacco control strategies, which set out their commitment to working with the UK Government to tackle illicit trade in tobacco. The present study mainly focuses on England.

2.4.1 The Irish Border

For historical reasons, the Irish border is a matter of great political, security, and diplomatic sensitivity.[32] This issue has dominated talks for months in the context of Brexit and the word 'backstop' has become common parlance in the UK and beyond. Generally used to describe a position of last resort, 'backstop' in the context of Brexit means maintaining a seamless border on the island of Ireland in the event of a *'Hard Brexit'*. To prevent the reintroduction of a physical border with physical checks and infrastructure between Ireland and the UK, the latter had suggested that technological solutions could provide a 'non-visible border'. Such claims were met with scepticism in Brussels.[33] The backstop negotiated by former PM May implied a single customs territory, effectively keeping the whole of the UK (and not only Northern Ireland) in the EU customs union unless and until both the EU and UK decide otherwise.

The 2019 Withdrawal Agreement negotiated by PM Johnson largely reflects what was done by his predecessor but departs from it on the crucial backstop issue. To appease hard-line Brexiteers, a complex new mechanism was agreed.

The new approach foresees that customs controls will happen when goods arrive to Northern Ireland, rather than across the island of Ireland. In practice, as illustrated in Art. 5 of the *Protocol on Ireland/Northern Ireland to the 2019 Withdrawal Agreement*, the actual checks will be on what is effectively a customs border between Great Britain and the Island of Ireland, with goods being checked at 'points of entry' in Northern Ireland. In other words, while legally there will be a customs border between Northern Ireland (which stays in the UK) and the Republic of Ireland (which stays in the EU), in practice goods will not be checked on the border between them but rather at ports and airports in Northern Ireland. Tariffs will only have to be paid on goods being moved from Great Britain to Northern Ireland if those products are considered 'at

---

[32] After decades of unrest, the Northern Ireland peace process led to the adoption of the Good Friday Agreement (or Belfast Agreement), effective from 2 December 1999. Among other things, the Agreement sets out the present devolved system of government and creates a number of institutions between Northern Ireland and the Republic of Ireland and between the latter and the UK. Recitals in the Protocol on Ireland/Northern Ireland of the 2019 Withdrawal Agreement states *"recalling that the United Kingdom's withdrawal from the Union presents a significant and unique challenge to the island of Ireland, and reaffirming that the achievements, benefits and commitments of the peace process will remain of paramount importance to peace, stability and reconciliation there"*.
[33] See Rice (2019), and Tidey (2019).

risk' of being transported into the Republic of Ireland. A joint committee made up of UK and EU representatives will draw up a list of what goods are considered 'at risk'. If tariffs are paid on 'at risk' goods that do not end up being sent on from Northern Ireland into the EU, the UK would be responsible for refunding the relevant amounts.

Furthermore, pursuant to Art. 8 of the *Protocol on Ireland/Northern Ireland to the 2019 Withdrawal Agreement*, EU law on value added tax will apply in Northern Ireland, but will be limited to goods (not services). Accordingly, Northern Ireland will be allowed to have different VAT rates than the rest of the UK, which would not normally be allowed under EU law. This means that Northern Ireland may apply the same VAT rates on certain goods as the Republic of Ireland, to stop any unfair advantages on either side of the border that could be exploited by illicit activities.

Several commentators voiced their concerns for increased illicit trade following Brexit between the Republic of Ireland—an EU Member—and Northern Ireland.[34] The Irish border has a history of smuggling activities. Illicit trade seems to concentrate on tobacco products and fuel. HMRC considers the smuggling of counterfeit cigarettes—manufactured in Eastern Europe and Asia—into Ireland and across the border as a significant threat.[35] Also, Irish authorities have reported a number of illicit production facilities producing counterfeit cigarettes for the UK market.[36] The risk of increased illicit activities around the Irish border will depend on the final outcome of the negotiations between the UK and the EU. While the excise tax differential between the UK and Ireland is minimal—both countries apply excise tax rates that are among the highest in the EU—the possible introduction of import tariffs on tobacco products imported into the UK from the EU (a scenario conceivable under the '*Hard Brexit*' scenario) could work as additional incentive to pursue illicit activities targeting the UK. This aspect is discussed in Sect. 4.1.1 below.

2.4.2 Gibraltar

Gibraltar has been under British control since 1713. Its status as an overseas territory has long been a source of contention with Spain, and the latter threatened to use its veto over Britain's divorce deal unless some of its demands were met. Spain used Brexit to secure measures to combat tobacco smuggling. Indeed, the region has traditionally been the entry point for illegal tobacco products into Spain. In 2017,

---

[34] See for instance, Jones (2019). https://www.irishtimes.com/news/ireland/irish-news/smuggling-at-the-border-why-the-uk-s-brexit-plan-is-raising-fears-1.3,824,760https://www.irishtimes.com/news/ireland/irish-news/smuggling-at-the-border-why-the-uk-s-brexit-plan-is-raising-fears-1.3824760.

[35] Police Service of Northern Ireland and An Garda Siochana (2018) Cross Border Organised Crime Assessment 2018.

[36] Ibid.

2.4 Territorial Impact

Spanish authorities seized more than 600,000 cartons of cigarettes.[37] Figures show that the discrepancy between consumption of licit tobacco products and legitimate imports is substantial, with part of the difference presumably diverted toward the illicit market.[38] Significant price differences create opportunities for arbitrage that can be exploited.

The territorial status of Gibraltar within the EU is peculiar.[39] Gibraltar is a VAT free jurisdiction.[40] Since it is outside the customs union and Schengen Area, contrary to the Irish border, Gibraltar already has a relatively 'hard' border with Spain, with the result that checks were required on goods and people crossing to and from Spain. At the request of Spain, the UK negotiated a specific *Protocol on Gibraltar to the 2018 Withdrawal Agreement* with several references to illicit trade, specifically in tobacco products (see Sect. 2.2.1. above).[41] Further, the UK and Spain signed the *Memorandum of Understanding on Tobacco and other Products* and several other bilateral instruments.[42] The entry into force of such memoranda is subject to the ratification of the 2019 Withdrawal Agreement in the UK and the EU.

The main goal of the *Memorandum of Understanding on Tobacco and other Products* is to limit the price differences between tobacco products sold in Spain and those sold in Gibraltar where they are much cheaper, and therefore to reduce arbitrage opportunities. According to Paragraph 1 on 'Price Differentials':

> The Government of Gibraltar, being concerned about […] the existence of an illicit trade in tobacco in the area around Gibraltar […] has committed to ensure that, by 30th June 2020 the average retail price differential of tobacco products (cigarettes, cigars, fine cut tobacco, and other tobacco products) will be no more than 32% greater than the most recently published Spanish prices for the equivalent tobacco products in mainland Spain and the Balearics. […] For cigarette products the market will be divided into four categories of product: premium cigarettes, mid-high cigarettes, mid-low cigarettes and lower-price cigarettes with a minimum price provided for each category. For fine cut tobacco, the market will be divided into two categories of product: premium and non-premium with a minimum price provided for each category. The Gibraltarian competent authorities will set minimum retail prices for each of the categories of tobacco products, which will be published quarterly in the Gibraltar Gazette. […]

---

[37] See, for instance, de Miguel and Abellan (2018).

[38] Gibraltar imported 72 million packs of cigarettes in 2017 despite its meagre population of just 34,000 inhabitants, according to the Spanish Tax Agency. If all of the tobacco imported went on internal consumption it would mean each Gibraltarian would have to smoke 5.8 packs of cigarettes every day. See, for instance, The Olive Press (2018).

[39] The UK is responsible for Gibraltar's external relations and Union law is applicable to Gibraltar to the extent provided in the 1972 Act of Accession by virtue of Article 355(3) TFEU.

[40] The UK's 1972 Act of Accession provided for certain derogations in relation to Gibraltar, including exclusion from the Common Agricultural and Fisheries Policies, and from the customs union (including VAT and common commercial policies).

[41] In general, on the Protocol and on the negotiations between Spain and the UK, see Durrant et al. (2018).

[42] HM Government (2018) Brexit negotiations: Gibraltar Memoranda of Understanding.

The Memorandum also contains provisions on information sharing, according to which the Parties undertake to exchange detailed information, for instance regarding the amount of raw or unmanufactured tobacco and tobacco products that have been imported, sold or exported from or to Gibraltar, details of imports, specifying variety, origin, exporter, destination, importer, and weight in kilogrammes (for raw or unmanufactured tobacco). For tobacco products, information will distinguish between the different types of tobacco products, report on the trend in retail prices for each tobacco product type (weighted average price for the amount sold, minimum price and maximum price).[43] With regard to enforcement, the Memorandum mandates reciprocal cooperation, in particular for the identification of persons responsible for smuggling activities and for the collection of debts owed to the state.[44]

References

Brown C (2019) Polls close in historic British election. CBC News, 12 Dec 2019. https://www.cbc.ca/news/world/britain-brexit-election-johnson-corbyn-vote-1.5392818. Accessed 24 February 2020

Consolidated version of the Treaty on European Union (TEU). OJ C 326, 26.10.2012, pp 13–390. https://eur-lex.europa.eu/legal-content/EN/TXT/?uri=celex%3A12012M%2FTXT. Accessed 24 Feb 2020

Council of the European Union (2011) Council Directive 2011/64/EU of 21 June 2011 on the structure and rates of excise duty applied to manufactured tobacco, OJ L 176, p 24, 5 July 2011

Crawford R (2018) We need 5000 extra customs officers to cope with Brexit—but more cuts are coming instead

de Miguel B and Abellan L (2018) Tobacco complicates Brexit negotiations with Gibraltar. El Pais online, 17 Oct 2018. https://elpais.com/elpais/2018/10/17/inenglish/1539760338_678882.html. Accessed 24 February 2020

Directive 2014/40/EU of the European Parliament and of the Council of 3 April 2014 on the approximation of the laws, regulations and administrative provisions of the Member States concerning the manufacture, presentation and sale of tobacco and related products and repealing Directive 2001/37/EC, OJ L 127, 29.4.2014

Durrant T, Stojanovic A, Lloyd L (2018) Negotiating Brexit: the views of the EU 27. Institute for Government, March 2018. https://www.instituteforgovernment.org.uk/sites/default/files/publications/IfG_views-eu-27-v5_WEB.pdf. Accessed 24 Feb 2020

EC-Turkey Association Council (1995). Decision No 1/95 of the EC-Turkey Association Council of 22 December 1995 on implementing the final phase of the Customs Union (96/142/EC). https://www.avrupa.info.tr/sites/default/files/2016-09/Custom_Union_des_ENG_0.pdf. Accessed 24 Feb 2020

---

[43] See Paragraph 2, Memorandum of Understanding on Tobacco and Other Products. The Memorandum also requires sharing information that distinguish between direct retail sales and duty-free sales to leisure cruises or other forms of transport (para. 2); and report, on a quarterly basis, about the effectiveness of the efforts made to prevent and combat fraud and smuggling in the region, including the legislation adopted for this purpose, the administrative and judicial measures applied, the human and material resources employed to combat fraud and smuggling, and the quantity and value of the seizures made (with specific reference to traceability).

[44] See Paragraph 5 and 6, Memorandum of Understanding on Tobacco and Other Products.

References

EFTA (2020) Basic features of the EEA agreement. https://www.efta.int/eea/eea-agreement/eea-basic-features. Accessed 24 Feb 2020

EU-Canada Comprehensive Economic and Trade Agreement (2017). https://ec.europa.eu/trade/policy/in-focus/ceta/. Accessed 24 Feb 2020

Euronews (2020) Post-Brexit guide: where are we now—and how did we get here? 25 February 2020. https://www.euronews.com/2020/02/11/brexit-draft-deal-first-of-many-hurdles-to-a-smooth-exit Accessed 27 Feb 2020

European Commission (2019) The EU-UK withdrawal agreement explained, 8 February 2019, TF50 (2019) 59. https://ec.europa.eu/commission/sites/beta-political/files/the_withdrawal_agreement_explained.pdf. Accessed 24 Feb 2020

European Communities Act 1972. United Kingdom Parliament. http://www.legislation.gov.uk/ukpga/1972/68/contents. Accessed 24 Feb 2020

European Union (Withdrawal) Act 2018. United Kingdom Parliament. http://www.legislation.gov.uk/ukpga/2018/16/contents/enacted. Accessed 24 Feb 2020

HM Government (2018) Agreement on the withdrawal of the United Kingdom of Great Britain and Northern Ireland from the European Union and the European Atomic Energy Community, as endorsed by leaders at a special meeting of the European Council on 25 November 2018. https://www.gov.uk/government/publications/withdrawal-agreement-and-political-declaration. Accessed 24 Feb 2020

HM Government (2018) Brexit negotiations: Gibraltar memoranda of understanding. https://www.gov.uk/government/publications/eu-exit-negotiations-gibraltar-memoranda-of-understanding. Accessed 24 Feb 2020

HM Government (2019) New withdrawal agreement and political declaration. https://www.gov.uk/government/publications/new-withdrawal-agreement-and-political-declaration. Accessed 24 Feb 2020

HM Government (2019) Political Declaration setting out the framework for the future relationship between the United Kingdom and the European Union, 19 Mar 2019. https://assets.publishing.service.gov.uk/government/uploads/system/uploads/attachment_data/file/840656/Political_Declaration_setting_out_the_framework_for_the_future_relationship_between_the_European_Union_and_the_United_Kingdom.pdf. Accessed 24 Feb 2020

Jones JH (2019) Smuggling at the border: why the UK's Brexit plan is raising fears. Irish Times, 14 March 2019. https://www.irishtimes.com/news/ireland/irish-news/smuggling-at-the-border-why-the-uk-s-brexit-plan-is-raising-fears-1.3824760. Accessed 24 Feb 2020

Milliken D, John M (2019) UK heading for 'fairly hard' Brexit if Johnson deal passes. Reuters, 18 October 2019. https://ru.reuters.com/article/idUSKBN1WW2F8. Accessed 24 Feb 2020

National Audit Office (2017) The UK border: issues and challenges for government's management of the border in light of the UK's planned departure from the EU. Session 2017–2019, HC 513, National Audit Office, October 2017. www.nao.org.uk/wp-content/uploads/2017/10/The-UK-border.pdf. Accessed 24 Feb 2020

National Audit Office (2018) The UK border: preparedness for EU exit. HC 1619 Session 2017–2019 24 October 2018. https://www.nao.org.uk/wp-content/uploads/2018/10/The-UK-border-preparedness-for-EU-exit.pdf. Accessed 24 Feb 2020

O'Carrol L (2017) Concerns as HMRC faces 'fivefold rise in customs checks' after Brexit. The Guardian, 31 March 2017. https://www.theguardian.com/politics/2017/mar/31/uk-ports-struggling-fivefold-rise-customs-brexit-hmrc-mps-declaration. Accessed 24 Feb 2020

O'Carroll L (2019) Can UK get 'super Canada-plus' trade deal with EU by end of 2020? The Guardian, 12 November 2019. https://www.theguardian.com/politics/2019/nov/12/can-uk-get-brexit-super-canada-plus-trade-deal-with-eu-by-end-of-2020. Accessed 24 Feb 2020

Office for National Statistics (2018) UK balance of payments, the pink book: 2018. https://www.ons.gov.uk/releases/ukbalanceofpaymentsthepinkbook2018. Accessed 24 Feb 2020

Police Service of Northern Ireland and An Garda Siochana (2018) Cross border organised crime assessment 2018. https://www.justice-ni.gov.uk/sites/default/files/publications/justice/cross-border-organised-crime-assessment-2018.PDF. Accessed 24 Feb 2020

Rice C (2019) Irish border: technology 'only part of solution' after Brexit. BBC Online, 26 June 2019. https://www.bbc.com/news/uk-northern-ireland-48772409. Accessed 24 Feb 2020

Sandford A (2018) No-deal Brexit: what would 'WTO terms' mean for UK-EU trade? Euronews, 31 July 2019. https://www.euronews.com/2018/12/19/how-would-uk-eu-trade-be-affected-by-a-no-deal-brexit. Accessed 24 Feb 2020

The Olive Press (2018) Spanish tax agency questions Gibraltar's Tobacco Imports. The Olive Press, 4 March 2018. https://www.theolivepress.es/spain-news/2018/03/04/spanish-tax-agency-questions-gibraltars-tobacco-imports/. Accessed 24 Feb 2020

The Tobacco products (traceability and security features) regulations (2019) United Kingdom Parliament. http://www.legislation.gov.uk/uksi/2019/594/made. Accessed 24 Feb 2020

Tidey A (2019) Irish border: can technology remove the need for a backstop? Euronews, 5 February 2019. https://www.euronews.com/2019/02/05/irish-border-can-technology-remove-the-need-for-a-backstop. Accessed 24 Feb 2020

TUC, 3 October 2018. https://www.tuc.org.uk/blogs/we-need-5000-extra-customs-officers-cope-brexit-more-cuts-are-coming-instead. Accessed 24 Feb 2020

UK Parliament (2017) Brexit: Gibraltar. House of Lords, European Union Committee, 13th Report of Session 2016–17 HL Paper 116. https://publications.parliament.uk/pa/ld201617/ldselect/ldeucom/116/116.pdf. Accessed 24 Feb 2020

UK Parliament (2017) European Union Committee Brexit: trade in goods. 16th Report of Session 2016–17. Published 14 March 2017—HL Paper 129. https://publications.parliament.uk/pa/ld201617/ldselect/ldeucom/129/12902.htm. Accessed 24 Feb 2020

UK in a Changing Europe (2018) EU-Turkey customs union. https://ukandeu.ac.uk/explainers/eu-turkey-customs-union/. Accessed 24 Feb 2020

UK in a Changing Europe (2019) The European single market. https://ukandeu.ac.uk/explainers/the-european-single-market/. Accessed 24 Feb 2020

UNCTAD (2019) No-deal Brexit: the trade winners and losers, 3 April 2019. https://unctad.org/en/pages/newsdetails.aspx?OriginalVersionID=2052. Accessed 24 Feb 2020

Ward M (2019) Statistics on UK-EU trade. House of Commons Library, Briefing Paper Number 7851, 24 July 2019. https://researchbriefings.parliament.uk/ResearchBriefing/Summary/CBP-7851#fullreport. Accessed 24 Feb 2020

Open Access This chapter is licensed under the terms of the Creative Commons Attribution 4.0 International License (http://creativecommons.org/licenses/by/4.0/), which permits use, sharing, adaptation, distribution and reproduction in any medium or format, as long as you give appropriate credit to the original author(s) and the source, provide a link to the Creative Commons license and indicate if changes were made.

The images or other third party material in this chapter are included in the chapter's Creative Commons license, unless indicated otherwise in a credit line to the material. If material is not included in the chapter's Creative Commons license and your intended use is not permitted by statutory regulation or exceeds the permitted use, you will need to obtain permission directly from the copyright holder.

Chapter 3
The Issue of Illicit Tobacco Trade in the UK

Illicit tobacco trade, as much as trade in other illicit products, is nothing new.[1] Some have argued that it has probably existed since the introduction of tobacco as a valuable and sought-after product from the New World. A lot has been written about the topic and tobacco remains among the most traded products on the illicit market.[2] Ultimately, illicit tobacco trade is the outcome of demand and supply. This is true for the UK as well. Consumers wish to save money, demanding cheaper or not available tobacco products, while illicit suppliers wish to make money and are thus interested in meeting demand to ensure larger sales, increased market shares, and greater profit. It is therefore generally accepted that only a combination of targeted policy and operational law enforcement measures addressing both supply and demand can stem illicit tobacco trade. This important premise underpins the holistic strategies implemented by the EU[3] and the UK[4] to counter illicit tobacco trade.

Assessing illicit tobacco trade is no easy task. As a clandestine activity by definition, illicit trade remains hidden until discovered. Experts have tried to estimate the impact of illicit tobacco at the global level. While acknowledging the difficulties related to the task, there appears to be a consensus which puts annual revenue loss in tobacco taxation worldwide at USD 40–50 billion, that is 600 billion sticks (individual cigarettes), equal to approximately 10% of global consumption.[5] The ever evolving and adapting nature of illicit trade makes it hard to accurately account for it. Yet, collating data is essential for understanding the size and nature of the problem,

---

[1] Tobacco is not the only product that suffers from illicit trade. Solutions and recommendations against illicit tobacco trade can, to some extent, also apply to other industries. Conversely, solutions already applied to other industries (for instance pharma, fashion or defence) can inspire the development of solutions for illicit tobacco trade as well.

[2] See, for instance, Allen (2017).

[3] OLAF (2018) New Action Plan reaffirms Commission in leading role in fight against cigarette smuggling.

[4] HMRC and UK Border Force (2015) Tackling illicit tobacco: From leaf to light The HMRC and Border Force strategy to tackle tobacco smuggling.

[5] World Bank (2019).

© The Author(s) 2020
M. Foltea, *Brexit and the Control of Tobacco Illicit Trade*,
SpringerBriefs in Law, https://doi.org/10.1007/978-3-030-45979-6_3

identifying and where possible anticipating emerging issues, devising countermeasures, and regularly assessing the effectiveness of the chosen strategy with a view to constantly refine and improve it.

3.1 Definition and Forms of Illicit Trade

Pursuant to Art. 1 (a) of the WHO FCTC, 'illicit trade' means *"any practice or conduct prohibited by law and which relates to production, shipment, receipt, possession, distribution, sale or purchase including any practice or conduct intended to facilitate such activity"*. Illicit trade can be undertaken both by illicit players who are not registered with the relevant government agencies, as well as by legitimate entities whose business operations are contrary to applicable laws and regulations. Illicit tobacco can derive from *illicit domestic production* or from *illicit imports*.

- *Illicit domestic production* is where tobacco products which are manufactured for consumption in the same jurisdiction are not declared to tax authorities. Products (which may be genuine or counterfeit) are sold without applicable taxes and may be manufactured in approved factories or as part of illegal covert operations.
- *Illicit imports* refer the unlawful movement of tobacco products from one tax jurisdiction to another without the payment of applicable taxes, or in breach of laws prohibiting their import or export.

Illegal imports involve products that can be genuine, counterfeit, or so-called 'cheap whites' or 'illicit whites'.[6] The illicit import of genuine products is often considered 'old school' large-scale cigarette smuggling, whereas counterfeit products are manufactured illegally—i.e. they bear a trademark without the owner (or authorized manufacturer's) consent. 'Cheap whites' or 'illicit whites' are terms used to describe cigarettes produced legally in one country, usually by smaller, low-profile businesses without trademark infringement, but have no legitimate market and are manufactured with the intent of being smuggled and sold outside of their country of production. Finally, illicit imports also include the abuse of legal privileges, i.e. situations where buyers/consumers exceed their allowances for imports of otherwise licit tobacco products.

These patterns, with some variations, apply to trade in all tobacco products, including cigarettes, hand rolling tobacco (HRT), and cigars. Illicit trade adjusts to the introduction of new legislation. Constantly seeking ways to circumvent control measures, it is receptive to new consumer trends and to new instruments and channels that can be used to reach customers. Like other activities, both licit and illicit, illicit tobacco traders are well aware of the business opportunities that the digital revolution offers. Social media, the growth of e-commerce, and the proliferation of postal and small parcel delivery services are revolutionizing the way consumers choose and purchase their favourite products. Unsurprisingly, these new trends are also having an impact

---

[6]See, for instance, Allen (2017).

on illicit trade in tobacco products. Small parcel delivery service in particular, has emerged as an issue of great concern. Already in 2016, a survey by the Organization for Economic Co-operation and Development (OECD) identified the growing volume of small parcels in the postal system as a *"major threat to the [authorities'] ability to combat illicit trade"*.[7] OECD and the European Union Intellectual Property Office (EUIPO) have also signalled how tobacco products are among the main fake product categories shipped via small parcels to the EU.[8]

Most trade in tobacco products is a perfectly licit (albeit tightly regulated and taxed) activity. Today, the UK has no commercial tobacco leaf production and its domestic manufacturing of cigarettes is marginal. The tobacco industry has been steadily reducing its workforce over several decades, largely as a result of mechanisation and rationalisation. The last two producers, Imperial Tobacco and Japan Tobacco International, closed their factories in Nottingham and in Northern Ireland in 2016 and 2017 respectively.[9] Absent domestic production, the licit tobacco market in the UK, for cigarettes and for other products, is comprised of imports. In 2018, the UK's top six import sources of tobacco products were all EU Member States, namely Poland, Germany, the Netherlands, Romania, and Belgium.[10]

Government data reports that in 2017, 28.6 billion sticks were released in the UK, a decrease from 2016 (30.9 billion) and 2015 (32.6 billion). Sales of cigarettes for home consumption have continued to fall since the mid-1990s and the quantity released in 2017 is 66% less than in 1996. Hand-rolled tobacco (HRT) shows an opposite trend. Since 1990, there has been an increase in the proportion of UK smokers using these products. Sales of HRT more than doubled between 2004 and 2012, reflecting the increase in the proportion of adults who smoked hand-rolled cigarettes. This trends remained fairly steady since 2012.[11]

3.2 The Duty-Free Regime (Personal Allowances)

Beside domestic sales, tobacco can be brought into the UK legally by consumers themselves (personal allowances). Currently, consumers do not pay duty or tax on tobacco products that they bring in from the EU if the following three conditions are cumulatively fulfilled: (1) the products are transported by the consumers; (2) the products are used by the consumers or given away as a gift; and (3) duty and tax have been paid in the EU country where consumers bought them. Although there

---

[7]OECD (2018) Governance Frameworks to Counter Illicit Trade, p. 79.

[8]OECD and EUIPO (2018) Misuse of Small Parcels for Trade in Counterfeit Goods: Facts and Trends.

[9]The two companies still dominate the licit cigarette market in the UK with a combined market share of around 80%.

[10]Statista.com (2019) Leading 5 importing countries of tobacco into the United Kingdom in 2018, ranked by value (in 1000 GBP).

[11]NHS (2018) Statistics on Smoking—England, 2018.

are no limits on the amount of tobacco that can be brought in from EU countries, since the goods are meant for self-consumption and not for resale, guide levels are provided to help customs officers distinguish between genuinely private imports and commercial importation. Border control is likely to enquire if the amounts carried exceed 800 cigarettes, 200 cigars, 400 cigarillos or 1 kg of tobacco per person.[12] For imports from non-EU Member States, the duty-free regime applies.[13] Accordingly, passengers traveling from non-EU Member States to the UK can bring in, without paying duty or tax, one of the following: 200 cigarettes, 100 cigarillos, 50 cigars, or 250 g tobacco.[14] Quantities that exceed the personal allowance have to be declared and are subject to applicable duties and taxes. The possible impact of Brexit on the personal allowances for tobacco products is presented in Sect. 4.1.1 below.

3.3 UK Illicit Tobacco Trade Data

Data on the illicit tobacco trade in the UK comes from two source—the UK government, and the tobacco industry itself. Trends from these two sources are reported in this section, along with a comparison with EU-wide trends.

3.3.1 UK Government Information

Illicit tobacco trade exists, as proven on the supply side by the regular seizure of tobacco products, and on the demand side by public perception surveys. According to the World Customs Organization (WCO), in 2017 customs officers from 91 countries provided data on 12,228 cases involving goods being smuggled to avoid excise taxes. Primarily, these goods were alcohol products and tobacco products, including cigarettes.[15] According to the 2016 survey commissioned by the European Anti-Fraud Office (OLAF) to Eurobarometer titled *'Public perception of illicit tobacco trade'*, 21% of the respondents in the UK revealed to have been offered black market cigarettes to smoke.[16] Estimating or even quantifying illicit markets, however, is methodologically challenging. Data provided by Government and private industry-commissioned initiatives do not always correspond.[17] Some commentators

---

[12]HM Government (2020) Bringing goods into the UK.

[13]Ibid.

[14]It is possible to split the allowance, e.g. 100 cigarettes and 25 cigars.

[15]In total, 14,786 seizures of alcohol, cigarettes, and other tobacco products were reported, with the recovery of 379,956,831 cigarette pieces, 468,778 cigars and 1,399,381.5 kg of other tobacco products. World Customs Organization (2017), p 147.

[16]EC Eurobarometer (2016a) Illicit Tobacco Trade—United Kingdom.

[17]The study Trajectory (2016), funded by SICPA, highlights how figures from different studies are at often odds.

3.3 UK Illicit Tobacco Trade Data

have criticized industry-commissioned studies, claiming that they overestimate illicit trade, feature substantial methodological problems, and fail to meet the standards of accuracy and transparency that are set by high-quality publications.[18]

For 2018, the UK Government estimates the illicit market share for cigarettes and HRT at 9% and 32%, respectively. There has been a clear downward trend from the all-time high reached in the 1990s, with the biggest drop occurring in the first decade of 2000. During that period, the illicit market share for cigarettes was nearly halved, decreasing from 22 to 12%. The illicit market share for HRT saw a decrease from 61 to 44% during the same period. For cigarettes, the decrease has been consistent, with only a few exceptions in 2012–2014 and again between 2016 and 2017. The reduction is confirmed in the 2017–2018 period, the most recent timeframe for which estimates are currently available, with a drop from 15% to 9% between the 2016–2017 and the 2017–2018 periods. Overall, the illicit market share for HRT, is also decreasing, although it still captures a significantly more important portion of the market than cigarettes, and in the most recent period it has registered a slight increase (from 27 to 32%).[19]

One of the most immediate and tangible consequences of illicit tobacco trade is the tobacco tax gap.[20] Data, covering the 2017–2018 period, estimates the tobacco tax gap at £1.8 billion. Cigarettes and HRT contribute to the tax gap with £1.0 billion and £0.8 billion, respectively. The cigarette tax gap has experienced a sharp decrease from the previous period (2016–2017), when it stood at £1.6 billion. The HRT tax gap on the contrary increased, although very modestly, from £0.7 to £0.8 billion in the 2017–2018 period. The tax gap tends to reflect the downward trend in the illicit cigarettes market share. For HRT the overall trend is also downward with a slight increase in the most recent years.[21]

3.3.2 Tobacco Industry Information

Non-governmental initiatives also collect and publish data on tobacco consumption and illicit tobacco trade estimates. For instance, according to the *2019 KPMG Stella Project*, total cigarette consumption in the UK for 2018 stood at 36.7 billion sticks (−2% compared to 2017). Illicit cigarettes, defined in the study as 'contraband and counterfeit (C&C)', amounted to 7.1 billion sticks (+0.2% compared to 2017), which is equal to 19.3% (+1.4% compared to 2017) of total consumption. The total tax revenue loss from illicit cigarettes in 2018 amounted to £2.772 million (+65 million from 2017). Both figures, are higher than the HMRC estimates presented above for the same year.

---

[18] See, for instance, Gallagher et al. (2019).
[19] NHS (2019) Statistics on Smoking—England, 2019.
[20] On the methods used by the UK Government to estimate illicit market shares and associated revenue losses. See World Bank (2019) pp. 188–189.
[21] NHS (2019) Statistics on Smoking—England, 2019.

The *Tobacco Manufacturers Association* (TMA) *Smokers' Anti-Illicit Trade Survey*, lastly conducted in 2018, highlights the attitudes, awareness, and understanding of smokers toward illicit tobacco in the UK.[22] The survey of over 12,000 adult smokers suggests that the number of smokers avoiding UK duty now stands at an all-time high, and that *"over three-quarters are regularly avoiding taxes by buying tobacco from the black market [illicit], abroad or duty free [licit as long as the personal allowances are not exceeded]"*. The findings also suggest that adult smokers are being pushed towards non-UK duty tobacco by high tobacco taxation, the introduction of plain packaging, and the recent ban on minimum tobacco pack sizes.[23]

With regard to the patterns of illicit trade, the data available is unanimous in concluding that, with the notable exception of Gibraltar, the UK is target market (ending point).[24] It is neither a transit or origin point. The 2018 KPMG's Stella Project found that, with the exception of Ukraine, inflows to the UK are principally from holiday destinations (Spain) and countries with large UK emigrant communities (Poland and Romania).[25]

Illegal cigarettes arrive in the UK mainly by water, motor vehicle, or air flight. Ports are crucial junctions for illicit trade in tobacco products and in particular those well connected with other transport infrastructures. According to the *2018 KPMG Stella Project*, the fact that volumes of illicit cigarettes seem to be higher in the North East of England may be explained by the fact that inflows may have originated through sea-ports.[26]

Information relating to seizures can help in understanding the patterns of illicit tobacco trade.[27] The Project SIA *'Seizure Insight Analysis, Tobacco Product seizures in the EU, Norway and Switzerland'*, launched in 2019 by KMPG and commissioned by Philip Morris International (PMI), collates valuable information on seizures of illicit tobacco products.[28] The study reported 1301 seizures in the UK in the 2015–2018 period. Ports were the most common seizure location whereas retail shops were

---

[22]TMA (2018) TMA Smokers' Anti-Illicit Trade Survey 2018: Attitudes, Awareness and Understanding. The Tobacco Manufacturers' Association (TMA) is the trade association for the UK tobacco industry. The TMA's members are British American Tobacco UK Ltd., Imperial Tobacco Ltd. and Gallaher Ltd. (a member of the Japan Tobacco Group of companies).

[23]TMA (2018) TMA Smokers' Anti-Illicit Trade Survey 2018: Attitudes, Awareness and Understanding.

[24]Calderoni et al. (2013).

[25]KPMG (2019b) Project Stella, Report for the United Kingdom.

[26]Ibid.

[27]While the data based on seizures is solid, using it to estimate the total size of the illicit tobacco market is risky as the exercise implies setting a rate of interception of smuggled products. Some observers have assumed that maybe 10% of the illicit trade is intercepted, although the effective interception rate is likely to be lower. See European Commission (2016).

[28]KPMG (2019a) Project SIA-Seizure Insight Analysis, Tobacco Product seizures in the EU, Norway and Switzerland.

3.3 UK Illicit Tobacco Trade Data

the most common seizure premise. During the same period, 473.9 million sticks were seized, with a median size of 10.5 thousand sticks per seizure. The total value of the products seized (cigarettes and raw tobacco) amounted to €642.5 million.[29]

The digital era is impacting illicit trade in tobacco products and the UK is no exception. Studies show how illicit tobacco products are distributed online through three main channels: social media platforms, purpose-built hosted websites, and online marketplaces.[30] In some instances, Facebook, Instagram and Snapchat have been used to market illicit products directly to consumers and organise face-to-face transactions.[31] The *modus operandi* is being studied. The information available suggests that online sellers are not necessarily the same individuals that bring illicit products into the UK. Illicit products are often brought into the country by organised criminal groups and subsequently supplied to smaller-scale vendors who then resell online.[32]

The magnitude of this phenomenon clearly emerges from *Operation Jasper*, a multi-agency effort launched in 2015 and led by the *National Markets Group for Intellectual Property Protection* with the participation of over 100 Trading Standards. *Operation Jasper* targets sellers of illicit goods on social media and markets including counterfeit and pirated goods offered on Facebook and Instagram. Since inception, it has led to 20,000 infringing listings being removed from Facebook, full profiles being closed, 120+ raid actions and investigations being commenced, and several thousand counterfeit and pirated products being seized.[33] The collected intelligence shows links between the online and offline sale of counterfeit and pirated goods, and permits the identification of solid connections between intellectual property crime and other forms of criminality. Such an approach also allows for the engagement of platform owners, such as Facebook, regarding the issue of criminal use of internet platforms. Beside social media, purpose-built hosted websites, created to sell illicit

---

[29] The study reports the top seizures. In 2017 more than 100 tonnes of imported raw tobacco uncovered during a nationwide investigation that centred on Lancashire, whereas in February of the same year, more than 50 tonnes of illicit rolling tobacco were seized from a factory in east Lancashire and in December 2017, 22 tonnes of illegal tobacco were seized while being smuggled into Hull dock, the tobacco was discovered in a HGV lorry that had arrived from Rotterdam. KPMG (2019a) Project SIA-Seizure Insight Analysis.

[30] Illicit trade in tobacco products on "darknet" in Europe seems marginal. Darknet markets consist of websites, which are in many ways similar to other online platforms that facilitate trade, such as eBay or Amazon. The key difference is the anonymity afforded by accessing darknet markets. The darknet is part of the deep web, the part of the internet that is not accessible by standard web browsers, but is used for storing encrypted data such as government files and personal banking records.

[31] Most sales organized over social media do not seem to involve the use of postal or parcel services and rather result in face-to-face transactions with payment made in cash. One could refer to this trend as "digitalization of street selling". Babuta et al. (2018), p. 17.

[32] Babuta et al. (2018), p. 18.

[33] UK-IPO (2018) IP Crime and Enforcement Report 2017–2018. See also The National Trading Standards (2016). The National Trading Standards eCrime Team (NTSeCT) has been set up by the National Trading Standards Board and by the Department of Business, Innovation and Skills to investigate online scams and rip-offs of national significance.

tobacco products online, offer customers the possibility to pay by credit card and organise delivery by post. A third channel is made of online marketplaces, such as eBay and Amazon.[34]

Recent studies also show how the use of postal and parcel services to import illicit tobacco products is perceived as a prevalent and growing issue in the UK. According to a 2018 study by the *Royal United Services Institute for Defence and Security Studies* (RUSI), online channels are not only used by opportunist individual sellers, but also by organised criminals with international contacts, access to a steady supply of illicit products, and sophisticated distribution networks. Social behaviour and falling prices offered by many delivery providers suggest that more and more illicit consignments (including tobacco products) are being sent through postal channels, hidden in plain sight among a sea of other packages.[35]

3.3.3 Comparison with EU-Wide Data

OLAF, the European Anti-Fraud Office, estimates that illicit trade in tobacco products at the EU level drains €10 billion from EU and Member State budgets every year.[36] Industry studies, such as the KPMG *Project Stella* commissioned by PMI, estimates illicit cigarette in the EU for the year 2018 at 8.6% of total consumption, representing 43.6 billion cigarettes.[37] This figure is comparable to the size of the total legal cigarette sales in the UK, Austria, and Denmark combined.

According to KPMG, overall illicit cigarette consumption levels remained stable compared to 2017.[38] However, the KPMG report found a more than 30% increase in counterfeit consumption—the largest amount recorded to date.[39] Among EU countries, the UK has the largest counterfeit cigarette volumes (0.9 billion cigarettes) after Greece (1.5 billion cigarettes). Two additional findings of the study are that non-EU countries remain the largest source of illicit cigarettes consumed in the EU—with a reduced incidence of illicit cigarette consumption in EU Eastern border countries—suggesting that law enforcement activities in those areas are bearing fruit.

---

[34] Babuta et al. (2018).

[35] Ibid.

[36] OLAF (2018) New Action Plan reaffirms Commission in leading role in fight against cigarette smuggling. However, a comprehensive and accurate picture of the illicit tobacco market is missing at EU level. To assist in improving strategic activities, in 2018 OLAF put out a tender for a study aimed at *"identifying an approach to measure the illicit market in tobacco products"*. The study commissioned shall present a *"reliable, robust, replicable and independent methodology which over time will provide a solid basis to analyse ongoing trends in the illegal tobacco market and respond effectively to anti-fraud requirements"*. https://etendering.ted.europa.eu/cft/cft-display.html?cftId=3253.

[37] Stop Illegal (2019) New KPMG report in the EU reveals largest increase of counterfeit cigarette consumption to date.

[38] Ibid.

[39] Ibid.

Consumption of legal non-domestic cigarettes grew by 10% in 2018, indicating that consumers purchased lower-priced products when travelling, rather than using the illicit market.[40]

At the EU level, smuggling of genuine product in large scale seizures has decreased in the past years. At the same time, *cheap whites* dominate large-scale seizures reported by Member States to OLAF.[41] While cigarettes accounted for 24% of all detained articles (not just tobacco) at the EU external border in 2016,[42] detected illicit tobacco production in the EU also seems to be on the rise. Illegal production has also been registered near the UK border. For instance, an illegal factory dismantled in March 2018 in neighbouring Ireland had the capacity to produce a quarter of a million cigarettes per hour, according to a press release by the Revenue Commissioners in Ireland.[43] A 2016 survey commissioned by OLAF to Eurobarometer titled *Public perception of illicit tobacco trade*, reveals that 19% of the respondents on a EU-wide basis have been offered black market cigarettes to smoke.[44] The figure is slightly below that the average reported in the UK (21%).

The data presented shows that today, the UK is a target country for the purpose of illicit trade in tobacco products. The country has only marginal domestic manufacturing capacity—both licit and illicit—and thus does not represent an important point of origin for illicit tobacco. Likewise, current data does not highlight situations where the UK territory is used as transit for illicit tobacco products from third countries *en route* to the markets of other EU countries. The analysis of the impact of Brexit on illicit trade thus focuses chiefly on the UK market, rather than that of the EU.

References

Allen E (2017) The illicit trade in tobacco products and how to tackle it, 2nd edn. International Tax and Development Center (ITIC), World Customs Journal Report
Babuta A, Haenlein C, Reid A (2018) E-commerce, delivery services and the illicit tobacco trade. Royal united services institute for defence and security studies (RUSI). https://www.rusi.org/sites/default/files/20181016_ecommerce_delivery_services_illicit_tobacco_trade_web.pdf. Accessed 24 Feb 2020
Calderoni F, Favarin S, Ingrascì O, and Smit A (2013) The Factbook on the illicit trade in tobacco products 1—United Kingdom. Transcrime. http://www.transcrime.it/pubblicazioni/the-factbook-on-the-illicit-trade-in-tobacco-products-1/. Accessed 24 Feb 2020
Euractiv (2018) OLAF: illicit cut tobacco is a significant and growing market. https://www.euractiv.com/section/economy-jobs/news/olaf-illicit-cut-tobacco-is-a-significant-and-growing-market/. Accessed 27 Feb 2020

---

[40] Ibid.

[41] Euractiv (2018) OLAF: Illicit cut tobacco is a significant and growing market.

[42] European Commission (2018) OLAF—Policy—Joint Customs Operations.

[43] Republic of Ireland Revenue Dept (2018) Revenue and An Garda Siochana dismantle illicit cigarette factory in Jenkinstown.

[44] EC Eurobarometer (2016b) Penetration of Cigarettes in the Black Market, United Kingdom.

EC Eurobarometer (2016a) Illicit tobacco trade—United Kingdom. European Commission Special Eurobarometer 443, July 2016. https://ec.europa.eu/anti-fraud/sites/antifraud/files/eb_illicit_tobacco_trade_united_kingdom_en.pdf. Accessed 24 Feb 2020

EC Eurobarometer (2016b) Penetration of cigarettes in the black market, United Kingdom. European Commission Special Eurobarometer 443, July 2016. https://ec.europa.eu/anti-fraud/sites/antifraud/files/eb_illicit_tobacco_trade_united_kingdom_en.pdf. Accessed 24 Feb 2020

European Commission (2016) Technical assessment of the experience made with the Anti-Contraband and Anti-Counterfeit agreement and general release of 9 July 2004 among Philip Morris International and affiliates, the Union and its Member States. Commission Staff Working document, Brussels, 24.2.2016. https://ec.europa.eu/anti-fraud/sites/antifraud/files/technical_assessment_pmi_24022016_en.pdf. Accessed 24 Feb 2020

European Commission (2018) OLAF—policy—joint customs operations. https://ec.europa.eu/anti-fraud/policy/joint-customs-operations-jco_en. Accessed 27 Feb 2020

Gallagher AWA, Evans-Reeves KA, Hatchard JL, Gilmore AB (2019) Tobacco industry data on illicit tobacco trade: a systematic review of exiting assessments. BMJ J Tobacco Control 28(3):334–345

HM Government (2020) Bringing goods into the UK. Her Majesty's Government. https://www.gov.uk/duty-free-goods/arrivals-from-eu-countries, and https://www.gov.uk/duty-free-goods/arrivals-from-outside-the-eu. Accessed 24 Feb 2020

HMRC and UK Border Force (2015) Tackling illicit tobacco: from leaf to light the HMRC and border force strategy to tackle tobacco smuggling. Government of the United Kingdom. https://assets.publishing.service.gov.uk/government/uploads/system/uploads/attachment_data/file/418732/Tackling_illicit_tobacco_-_From_leaf_to_light__2015_.pdf. Accessed 24 Feb 2020

KPMG (2019a) Project SIA-seizure insight analysis, tobacco product seizures in the EU, Norway and Switzerland. KPMG. https://home.kpmg/uk/en/home/insights/2019/01/project-sia-tobacco-product-seizures-in-europe.html. Accessed 24 Feb 2020

KPMG (2019b) Project Stella report for the United Kingdom, 2019. KPMG. https://www.stopillegal.com/docs/default-source/external-docs/kpmg-project-stella/uk.pdf. Accessed 24 Feb 2020

NHS (2018) Statistics on smoking—England, 2018. National health service digital. https://digital.nhs.uk/data-and-information/publications/statistical/statistics-on-smoking/statistics-on-smoking-england-2018. Accessed 24 Feb 2020

NHS (2019) Statistics on smoking—England, 2019. National health service digital. https://digital.nhs.uk/data-and-information/publications/statistical/statistics-on-smoking/statistics-on-smoking-england-2019. Accessed 24 Feb 2020

OECD (2018) Governance frameworks to counter illicit trade. Organisation of Economic Cooperation and Development Publishing

OECD and EUIPO (2018) Misuse of small parcels for trade in counterfeit goods: facts and trends. OECD Publishing. https://doi.org/10.1787/9789264307858-en

OLAF (2018) New action plan reaffirms commission in leading role in fight against cigarette smuggling. European Anti-Fraud Office, Press Release No. 13/2018. https://ec.europa.eu/anti-fraud/media-corner/news/07-12-2018/new-action-plan-reaffirms-commission-leading-role-fight-against_en. Accessed 24 Feb 2020

Republic of Ireland Revenue Dept (2018) Revenue and An Garda Siochana dismantle illicit cigarette factory in Jenkinstown, Co. Louth. Revenue Department of the Republic of Ireland, 15 Mar 2018. https://www.revenue.ie/en/corporate/press-office/press-releases/2018/pr-150318-illegal-cigarette-factory-jenkinstown-louth.aspx. Accessed 24 Feb 2020

Statista.com (2019) Leading 5 importing countries of tobacco into the United Kingdom in 2018, ranked by value (in 1000 GBP). https://www.statista.com/statistics/305181/uk-tobacco-imports-leading-5-countries-by-value/. Accessed 24 Feb 2020

Stop Illegal (2019) New KPMG report in the EU reveals largest increase of counterfeit cigarette consumption to date. Stop Illegal, 11 June 2019. https://www.stopillegal.com/blog/detail/new-

References

kpmg-report-in-the-eu-reveals-largest-increase-of-counterfeit-cigarette-consumption-to-date. Accessed 24 Feb 2020

The National Trading Standards (2016) Products worth millions seized in counterfeiting crackdown. National trading standard, 23 Dec 2016. https://www.nationaltradingstandards.uk/news/products-worth-millions-seized-in-counterfeiting-crackdown/. Accessed 24 Feb 2020

TMA (2018) TMA smokers' anti-illicit trade survey 2018: attitudes, awareness and understanding. Tobacco Manufacturers' Association. http://the-tma.org.uk/2018/08/20/survey-reveals-the-buying-of-untaxed-tobacco-hits-an-all-time-high-2/. Accessed 24 Feb 2020

Trajectory (2016) Turning point: insights into illicit tobacco in the UK. Trajectory, July 2016. https://trajectorypartnership.com/wp-content/uploads/2016/07/Trajectory-paper-Illicit-tobacco-trade-UK-060716.pdf. Accessed 24 Feb 2020

UK-IPO (2018) IP crime and enforcement report 2017–2018. United Kingdom intellectual property office. https://assets.publishing.service.gov.uk/government/uploads/system/uploads/attachment_data/file/740124/DPS-007593_IP_Crime_Report_2018_-_Web_v2.pdf. Accessed 24 Feb 2020

World Bank (2019) Confronting illicit tobacco trade—a global review of country experiences, United Kingdom. World Bank. http://pubdocs.worldbank.org/en/248361548435105081/WBG-Tobacco-IllicitTrade-UnitedKingdom.pdf. Accessed 24 Feb 2020

World Customs Organization (2017). 2017 illicit trade report. World customs organization. http://www.wcoomd.org/-/media/wco/public/global/pdf/topics/enforcement-and-compliance/activities-and-programmes/illicit-trade-report/itr_2017_en.pdf?db=web. Accessed 24 Feb 2020

Open Access This chapter is licensed under the terms of the Creative Commons Attribution 4.0 International License (http://creativecommons.org/licenses/by/4.0/), which permits use, sharing, adaptation, distribution and reproduction in any medium or format, as long as you give appropriate credit to the original author(s) and the source, provide a link to the Creative Commons license and indicate if changes were made.

The images or other third party material in this chapter are included in the chapter's Creative Commons license, unless indicated otherwise in a credit line to the material. If material is not included in the chapter's Creative Commons license and your intended use is not permitted by statutory regulation or exceeds the permitted use, you will need to obtain permission directly from the copyright holder.

Chapter 4
UK Relevant Legal and Enforcement Frameworks

Among dual markets (i.e. those where a licit and an illicit market for the same commodity exist), the tobacco market is one of the most tightly regulated. Tobacco consumption poses health problems that generate great costs to society and the economy. As set out in the 2017 document *'Towards a Smokefree Generation—A Tobacco Control Plan for England'* prepared by the UK Department of Health, the overall goal of tobacco control in the UK is to reduce smoking prevalence and the stated vision is to create a smoke-free generation.[1]

The first comprehensive UK tobacco policy document was released in 1998 under the title *'Smoking Kills'*,[2] whereas the first coordinated national response to illicit tobacco trade was introduced only a few years later in 2000.[3] Actions to tackle illicit tobacco trade are an essential part of the UK's tobacco control policy. Over the years, commitment to controlling the use of tobacco products as well as to fight illicit trade has not diminished, regardless of the political leadership. This may suggest that tackling illicit tobacco trade will remain a priority in the UK, irrespective of the outcome of Brexit.

The 2000 anti-smuggling strategy prioritised enforcement. Significant investments were made to tackle the problem at the source with interventions targeting the supply side to prevent illicit tobacco from entering into the UK.[4] For instance, one thousand frontline and investigative staff were added along with additional x-ray scanners to detect high-scale cigarette smuggling in freight. The introduction of fiscal

---

[1] The objectives of the tobacco control plan are to: reduce the number of 15 year olds who regularly smoke from 8 to 3% or less, reduce smoking among adults in England from 15.5 to 12% or less, reduce the inequality gap in smoking prevalence, between those in routine and manual occupations and the general population, and reduce the prevalence of smoking in pregnancy from 10.5 to 6% or less. The aim is to achieve these objectives by the end of 2022. See UK Department of Health (2017).

[2] UK Department of Health (1998) Smoking Kills. A White Paper on Tobacco.

[3] HM Customs and Excise and HM Treasury (2000) Tackling tobacco smuggling.

[4] Ibid.

marks on UK duty-paid products, and increased use of criminal and civil sanctions to deter smuggling and reduce its profitability were also among the measures adopted under the first strategy.

The UK approach to illicit tobacco trade proved successful over the years. As discussed above, since 2000 there has been a significant reduction in illicit product market share and lost revenue. However, the footprint of the UK illicit market is not immutable. The nature of the threat from tobacco smuggling has evolved since HMRC's first strategy in 2000. Over the years, the strategy has been reviewed and reinforced to more effectively meet the evolving challenges.[5] The current strategy *'Tackling illicit tobacco: From leaf to light'* was presented jointly by HMRC and UK Border Force in 2015. It aims at holding the illicit cigarette market share at or below 10%, and at containing the illicit market share for hand-rolling tobacco and reversing the recent upward trend.[6]

The possible impact of Brexit on illicit trade in tobacco products in both the UK and EU more widely can be analysed on the basis of the key features of the current 'pre-Brexit' approach to tobacco control. This approach includes an articulate legal framework, an institutional framework, and enforcement mechanisms. Particular consideration is given to those elements of the current approach that are directly linked to EU membership, to identify the additional regulatory flexibility and the risks that may result from Brexit.

4.1 Relevant Legal Framework

In order to assess the possible impact of Brexit on the control of illicit tobacco trade, it is necessary to consider tobacco-specific measures in the UK but also non-specific measures that may have a bearing on the availability of tobacco products.

4.1.1 Fiscal Measures

Taxation is a preeminent element of tobacco control and one of the most effective ways to reduce the prevalence of smoking, mitigate its consequential health harms, and progress towards a tobacco-free society. Some commentators have highlighted how high taxation indirectly supports the persistence of an illicit market, as high prices can push some smokers to switch to illicit or other tax-non-paid cigarettes.[7] Instead of lower tobacco consumption and higher government revenue, the higher taxes would thus mainly benefit those who circumvent them.

---

[5] World Bank (2019).
[6] HMRC and UK Border Force (2015).
[7] Bate et al. (2019). The study, based on a smokers' survey, finds that the illicit white market is supported by consumers' willing to purchase illicit products for their reduced prices.

4.1 Relevant Legal Framework

Tobacco products in the UK are expensive. At 219% of the EU average, the UK price level index (PLI) of tobacco is the highest among EU Member States.[8] According to the UK Office for National Statistics, in August 2019 the average price for a pack of 20 king size filter cigarettes in the UK was £10.77.[9] The 'affordability of tobacco' index has fallen over the past three decades.[10] On the basis of smokers' purchasing power, with very few exceptions, tobacco products are today more expensive in the UK than virtually anywhere else in the world.

Tobacco Products Duty

The high prices for tobacco products in the UK are the result of a combination of different taxes. The most important component of the total price is the *Tobacco Products Duty*, which alone represents 90% of all tobacco duty receipts.[11] Based on the *Tobacco Products Duty Act 1979* the duty is a form of excise duty, payable on tobacco products manufactured in the UK or imported into the UK.[12] The *Tobacco Products Duty* is payable on cigarettes, cigars, HRT, and other smoking tobacco— for example pipe tobacco, chewing tobacco, cigarette rag or expanded tobacco—if it can be smoked without further processing.[13] Notably, the *Tobacco Products Duty* does not apply to tobacco leafs (raw tobacco). Products become liable to the *Tobacco Products Duty* when they enter the UK from overseas or reach a smokable condition during manufacture (events known as 'duty points'). Products may be stored duty-suspended in approved excise warehouses. When goods are released from an excise warehouse for consumption, the excise duty must have been paid or accounted for before they leave the warehouse.

The rate of the *Tobacco Products Duty* (in force since 29 October 2018) varies depending on the tobacco product, as illustrated in Table 4.1. For HRT, cigars, and other smoking and chewing tobacco, the duty takes the form of a specific tax (specific amount per quantity). Cigarettes, since May 2017, are subject to a combination of specific and ad valorem tax (percentage of the product value) or to a *Minimum Excise Tax* (MET), whichever is higher.[14] The MET sets a minimum level of excise duty for any packet of cigarettes, i.e. a floor below which the tax on cigarettes cannot fall. MET was introduced with a view of reducing the availability of cheap cigarettes, which in turn encourages quitting, and to increasing tax revenues.

The EU does not have a direct role in collecting taxes or setting tax rates. The amount of tax each citizen pays is decided by EU Members' national governments, along with how the collected taxes are spent. To facilitate intra-EU business and

---

[8] Eurostat (2019)—Comparative price levels for food, beverages and tobacco.
[9] Office of National Statistics (2020).
[10] NHS (2018) Statistics on Smoking—England, 2018.
[11] HMRC produces monthly publications with official statistical data on the Tobacco Products Duty. See HM Revenue and Customs (2019a)—UK Tobacco Duty Statistics.
[12] Other regulated (or excisable) products include alcoholic beverages and fuel.
[13] See Tobacco Products (Descriptions of Products) Order 2003.
[14] HM Revenue and Customs (2019c) Guidance: Tobacco Products Duty rates—Minimum Excise Duty for cigarettes.

Table 4.1 Tobacco products duty rates

Type or product	Duty rate	Minimum excise tax (MET)
Cigarettes	Either £228.29 per 1000 cigarettes plus 16.5% of retail price	OR £293.95 per 1000 cigarettes
Hand rolling tobacco (HRT)	£234.65/kg	Not applicable
Cigars	£284.76/kg	Not applicable
Tobacco for heating	£234.65 per kg	Not applicable
Other smoking and chewing tobacco	£125.20/kg	Not applicable

avoid competitive distortions, Member States have nevertheless agreed to align their rules for taxing goods and services, for instance in case of excise taxes, including on tobacco products and to some extent, for VAT.

In the area of excise duties, EU law provides for horizontal rules to cover, for example, the categories of products that Member States must apply excise duties to, the principles on where excise duty revenue accrues, and the rules on the production, storage and movement of excise products. Such common provisions, which apply to all products subject to excise duties under EU law, are set out in *Council Directive 2008/118/EC of 16 December 2008 concerning the general arrangements for excise duty and repealing Directive 92/12/EEC*.

Beside these common provisions for excisable goods, specific EU legislation on excise duties for manufactured tobacco is contained in *EU Directive 2011/64/EU on the structure and rates of excise duty applied to manufactured tobacco* (Tobacco Tax Directive). The Tobacco Tax Directive sets out the details of how tobacco products shall be taxed within the EU, mainly by providing the categories of manufactured tobacco products (cigarettes and 'other tobacco products'), the principles of taxation, as well as the minimum rates and structures to be applied. In the case of cigarettes, the Tobacco Tax Directive establishes a minimum rate which must consist of a specific component of between 7.5% and 76.5% of the total tax burden (TTB)—expressed as a fixed amount per 1000 cigarettes, and an *ad valorem* component—expressed as a percentage of the maximum retail selling price. In addition, the overall excise rate must be at least €90 per 1000 cigarettes and at least 60% of the weighted average retail selling price (Member States that apply excise duty of €115 or more, however, do not need to comply with this 60% criterion).

For other tobacco products, the Tobacco Tax Directive introduces a slightly different taxing structure. Member States can choose between applying a specific component or an ad valorem component, or if they wish, they may apply a mixture of the two. Minimum rates are set out for three distinct categories of 'other tobacco products': (i) for 'fine-cut smoking tobacco', 48% of the weighted average retail selling price or €60/kg; (ii) for 'cigars and cigarillos', 5% of the retail selling price or €12 per 1000 pieces or per kg; and (iii) for 'other smoking tobaccos', 20% of the retail selling price or €22/kg.

4.1 Relevant Legal Framework

EU legislation sets and regularly updates the harmonised minimum rates.[15] Member States are free to apply excise duty rates above the minima foreseen in the Tobacco Tax Directive. Excise duties in the UK are significantly higher than the minimum limits requested by the EU and there is a commitment to increase them annually by 2% above inflation for the duration of the current Parliament.[16]

Under all four Brexit scenarios analysed, post-Brexit UK would no longer be bound to excise minima foreseen in the EU legislation. In theory, the UK could therefore choose to apply lower excise duty rates. Since the Tobacco Products Duty represents the most important component of the total retail price of tobacco in the UK, a high diferential compared to neighbour countries could create an incentive for illicit activities. This may be the case with respect to the neighbouring Ireland, where retail prices are now by and large aligned with those in the UK.

Excise Movement and Control System (EMCS)
Closely linked to excise duties is the EU-wide Excise Movement and Control System (EMCS). Within the EU, excise taxes are paid in the country of final consumption. Established by *EU Directive 2008/118*,[17] the EMCS is a computerized, paperless system that is used by businesses when moving duty-suspended excise goods (alcohol, tobacco, and certain mineral oils) between EU Member States as part of their commercial activities. The system records in real time the movement of tobacco and other excise products for which excise duties still have to be paid, and helps to ensure that the appropriate duties are paid at the final destination. The authorised warehouse-keeper in the Member State of departure must provide a guarantee for the excise goods they dispatch, under duty-suspension, to another Member State, until the excise duty has been secured ('Report of Receipt' has been received) in the Member State of destination. As a standardized, electronic system for the whole EU, the EMCS also simplifies procedures and reduces administrative costs for businesses and tax authorities.

The purpose of the EMCS is to combat fiscal fraud by providing tax authorities and the involved traders with real-time information and checks on individual consignments of excise goods along the supply chain.[18] EMCS thus also helps to prevent illicit trade by monitoring the movement of excise goods within the EU until

---

[15] See European Commission (2019) Excise Duty Tables—Manufactured Tobacco. https://ec.europa.eu/taxation_customs/sites/taxation/files/resources/documents/taxation/excise_duties/tobacco_products/rates/excise_duties-part_iii_tobacco_en.pdf.

[16] Office for Budget Responsibility (2019) OBT Tobacco Duties.

[17] Council Directive 2008/118/EC of 16 December 2008 concerning the general arrangements for excise duty and repealing Directive 92/12/EEC.

[18] See European Commission (2020a) Excise Movement and Control System, and HM Revenue and Customs (2009) Guidance—Excise Movement and Control System: how to register and use.

the duties are paid or the goods are exported. The EU Commission's '*2nd Action Plan to fight illicit tobacco trade 2018–2022*' makes several references to this system.[19]

In principle, following Brexit implementation (regardless of its form), the EMCS would no longer be used to control suspended movements between the EU and the UK. The *2019 Withdrawal Agreement* only clarifies how to treat the movement of excise goods under duty suspension which started before the end of the transition period (which at the date of writing will end on 31 December 2020 unless extended).[20]

Both the UK and the EU prepared guidance notes for the movement of excise goods in the event of a '*Hard Brexit*'. Previous versions have in the meantime been withdrawn. The current guidance note explains how imports of excise goods from the EU to the UK will be treated from 1 January 2021.[21] After Brexit day, imports of excise duty-suspended goods to the UK from EU Member States will be treated in the same way as imports from the rest of the world. Businesses will no longer be able to use the EMCS to move excise duty-suspended goods to the UK from the EU. However, the EMCS would continue to be used to control the movement of duty suspended excise goods within the UK, including movements to and from UK ports, airports and the Channel tunnel.

Personal Allowance

Each EU country can decide on a maximum amount of tobacco products and alcoholic beverages that travellers are entitled to bring into the country as a *personal allowance*, i.e. products purchased are for personal use (own consumption or to be given away as gifts) and not for resale. Taxes (VAT and excise) are included in the price of the product in the country where they are purchased, so no further payments are due in any other EU country. Pursuant to *EU Directive 2008/118 concerning the general arrangements for excise duty*, the EU only establishes minimum guide levels or 'Minimum Indicative Limits (MILs)', for imports from EU countries ('EU allowance').[22] The MILs are as follows: 800 cigarettes, 200 cigars, 400 cigarillos, and 1 kg of tobacco.

As discussed in Sect. 3.2 above, today different limits apply for travellers to the UK from an EU country and travellers from third countries. Travellers from third countries can benefit from the 'international duty free allowance' based on *Council Directive 2007/74/EC of 20 December 2007 on the exemption from value added tax and excise duty of goods imported by persons travelling from third countries*.[23]

---

[19] European Commission (2018a) Annex to the Communication from the Commission to the European Parliament, the Council and the European Economic and Social Committee 2nd Action Plan to fight the illicit tobacco trade.

[20] Art. 52 and 53 of the 2019 Withdrawal Agreement.

[21] HM Revenue and Customs (2019d) UK Government Guidance—Importing excise goods to the UK from the EU from 1 January 2021.

[22] See Art. 32 'Acquisition by private individuals' of the Council Directive 2008/118/EC (concerning the general arrangements for excise duty).

[23] Council Directive 2007/74/EC of 20 December 2007 on the exemption from value added tax and excise duty of goods imported by persons travelling from third countries. See also UK The Travellers' Allowances (Amendment) Order 2008.

4.1 Relevant Legal Framework

Although less generous in terms of allowed quantity, in terms of prices, products under the international duty-free allowance are cheaper than those within the current EU allowance as they are 'duty-free' in the countries where they are purchased. The international duty-free allowance is as follows: 200 cigarettes, 50 cigars, 100 cigarillos, and 250 grams of tobacco.

Some have suggested that after Brexit, duty-free status for imports from EU Member States could be introduced, in lieu of the current EU allowances.[24] Under all four Brexit scenarios analysed, the UK would be free to depart from EU legislation regarding EU allowances or the international duty-free allowances, discussed above. Under a *'Hard Brexit'* scenario, this could happen immediately, without waiting until the end of the transition period. Because of its popularity among parts of the population, the issue of the reintroduction of duty free allowances on tobacco and alcoholic beverages for travellers from EU countries has been widely publicised and used by the Government to counter some of the negative stories surrounding a *'Hard Brexit'* with examples of how consumers will see some tangible and immediate benefits.[25] The adoption of more restrictive amendments could create incentives for consumers to consider cheaper products in the illicit market.

Value-Added Tax

A *value-added tax (VAT)* applies to all tobacco products. Since 2011, the standard VAT rate in the UK has been 20%.[26] VAT is administered and collected by HMRC. In the area of VAT, EU law requires Member States to have a single value-added tax rate of at least 15%. In addition to this rate, Member States can foresee no more than two reduced value-added tax rates set of no lower than 5%.[27]

After Brexit, the UK will no longer be bound by the minimum rates set by the EU. Under the different post-Brexit scenarios, such as a participation in the Customs Union, for instance following the precedent of Turkey,[28] or by remaining in the single market as in the EEA,[29] the UK would not be bound by EU legislation in the area of VAT. The same applies in case future UK-EU relations would be governed by a free trade agreement.

The *2019 Withdrawal Agreement* contains limited references to VAT. However, Art. 51 (Value added tax (VAT)) clarifies the regime applicable to goods travelling across borders during the transition period as well as the extent to which the EU VAT Directive shall continue to apply after the end of the transition period (set to last until 31 December 2020). Although there have been no discussions so far on amending VAT rates following Brexit, changes could occur. A different rate than what applies

---

[24] See for instance, Calder (2019) or Dathan (2019).

[25] See, for instance, Elliott (2019).

[26] Value Added Tax Act 1994.

[27] Council Directive 2006/112/EC (on the common system of value added tax), and Council Directive 2010/88/EU (amending Directive 2006/112/EC).

[28] In the case of Turkey, Turkey's VAT adaption progress has been evaluated annually by the European Commission since 1998, mainly because of the country's membership candidacy.

[29] In general, the EC rules on harmonisation of taxes are outside the scope of the EEA Agreement. The EU VAT Directive and other acts on taxation have not been incorporated into the EEA Agreement.

today would have an impact on the final price of tobacco products and thus on the attractiveness of illicit products. While changes could be sweeping or minimal, it seems highly unlikely that the Government will do away with VAT altogether as it represents a valuable source of revenue.

According to HMRC's *Notice—VAT for businesses*,[30] *in the event that the UK leaves the EU without an agreement*, the VAT rules relating to UK domestic transactions will continue to apply to businesses as they do now. The UK Government intends to keep VAT procedures as close as possible to what they are now.[31] Pursuant to Art. 8 of the revised Protocol, Northern Ireland will be allowed to have different VAT rates to the rest of the UK. In practice, this means that Northern Ireland may apply the same VAT rates on certain goods as the Republic of Ireland in order to stop an unfair advantage on either side of the border that could be exploited also by illicit activities.

4.1.2 Import Duties

Before excise duties and VAT, imported tobacco products may be subject to *import tariffs*. Today, the UK (and obiously so) does not levy any import duties on tobacco originating from EU Member States. The same applies to products from countries with whom the EU has concluded a preferential trade agreement (or that benefit from the Generalized System of Preferences) although in some cases, rather than a zero tariff, such agreements foresee lower (preferential) import tariffs than what applies to imports from third countries.[32]

As a result of the UK's participation in the EU Customs Union, the tariff rates currently applied by the UK on tobacco products as well as on any other products, are based on the EU Common Customs Tariff. The tariff rate depends on the origin of the imported product. *Ad valorem customs duties* are levied on importer's CIF (cost, insurance and freight) value. The UK currently applies import tariffs on tobacco products from *third countries*[33] as illustrated in Table 4.2.

---

[30] For reference, see Stuttaford and Brain (2018) VAT for businesses if there's no Brexit deal.

[31] Leaving the EU would nevertheless mean foregoing some of the current simplifications. For instance, goods moved from one EU country to another by a business registered for VAT in the UK is currently VAT-free for the UK business under a simplification known as triangulation. After exit, UK businesses can no longer expect to benefit from this EU simplification and instead can expect to be required to register for VAT within the EU. A further EU simplification is distance selling of goods. Small amounts of sales to customers in other EU countries do not require the supplier to register for VAT in the customer's country. If the UK is no longer part of the EU, either the customer will be responsible for import VAT and import duty, or the UK company will be required to register for VAT in the customer's EU country.

[32] The following database provides the complete list of countries with whom the EU has concluded a trade agreement and the applicable tariff rates https://www.trade-tariff.service.gov.uk/sections.

[33] HM Government (2020)—Trade Tariff Database.

4.1 Relevant Legal Framework

Table 4.2 Import tariffs on tobacco products from third countries

Type or product	Tariff (%)
Cigars, cheroots and cigarillos, containing tobacco (HS code 2402100000)	26.00
Cigarettes containing tobacco (HS code 2402209000)	57.60
Smoking tobacco whether or not containing tobacco substitutes in any proportion (HS code 240311), including loose hand-rolling and pipe tobacco or for use with a hookah or water pipe	74.90

Brexit could have an impact on import tariffs for tobacco products. As discussed above, most licit imports of tobacco product come from EU Member States. If, after Brexit implementation, the UK remains part of the EU Customs Union (i.e. the second scenario) building on the arrangement negotiated by former PM Theresa May, imports from the EU would continue to be duty free and imports from non-EU countries would be subject to the EU Common Customs Tariff. In case of relations based on a free trade agreement, one can expect tobacco products to be among the tariff lines for which import duties are equal to zero or at any other preferential level. In case of '*Hard Brexit*', however, the UK would in principle have to apply to imports from the EU, the same tariffs it applies to third countries—the so called '*WTO rate*' or '*MFN rate*'—which for cigarettes currently amounts to 57.60%. In preparation for Brexit, the UK Government has published a list of tariffs that would apply for imports in case the UK leaves the EU without an agreement for an initial period of up to 12 months.[34]

The World Trade Organization's Most Favoured Nation (MFN) obligation prevents WTO Members from applying to imports from one country, treatment more favourable than that provided for like product imports from other WTO Members.[35] Only the conclusion of a preferential trade agreement with the EU would allow the UK to apply preferential (even 'zero') tariffs to tobacco products from the EU, as it was the case previously under several preferential agreements that applied to the UK as part of its EU membership.[36] In the past few months, the UK has negotiated the 'rolling over' of a number of preferential trade agreements concluded by the EU with third countries. As of October 2019, the list of such agreements included *Israel, Switzerland, Chile, the Faroe Island, the Eastern and Southern Africa States (the Union of Comoros, the Republic of Madagascar, the Republic of Mauritius, the Republic of Seychelles, the Republic of Zambia and the Republic of Zimbabwe), the Palestinian Authority, Fiji and Papua New Guinea, CARIFORUM (Antigua and Barbuda, Barbados, Belize, The Commonwealth of Dominica, The Dominican Republic, Grenada,*

---

[34] See HM Government (2019a) Guidance—Check temporary rates of customs duty (tariffs) on imports after Brexit. The temporary rates of customs duty (tariffs) on imports would not apply to goods crossing from Ireland into Northern Ireland. At the WTO, the United Kingdom will make a further notification concerning the date of application of the draft Schedule *XIX-United Kingdom*. Until that date, the United Kingdom continues to be covered by the Schedule *CLXXV-European Union* (EU-28).
[35] See GATT Art. I.
[36] See GATT Art. XXIV.

The Republic of Guyana, Jamaica, Saint Christopher and Nevis, Saint Lucia, Saint Vincent and the Grenadines, The Republic of Trinidad and Tobago), Iceland and Norway, the Andean countries (Colombia, Peru, Ecuador), South Korea, as well as Central America (Costa Rica, El Salvador, Guatemala, Honduras, Nicaragua and Panama).[37] For imports from these countries, a preferential duty rate already applies to products that satisfy the rules of origin set out in the respective agreements.[38]

In a 2017 position paper, the Tobacco Manufacturers Association (TMA) suggested that the introduction of tariffs on imports of tobacco from the EU following Brexit would push up tobacco prices, thus exacerbating illicit trade.[39] In its statements, the TMA also stressed the fact that the UK has no tangible domestic tobacco manufacturing to protect from foreign competitors, and that the already significant tax burden weighs on the sector.[40]

To put things in perspective, in the 2017–2018 period HMRC collected a total of £3.4 billion in import tariffs on goods brought into the UK.[41] Contrary to excise taxes, import tariffs are not aimed at influencing consumers' behaviour. Their purpose is to increase the cost of imported goods in order to benefit domestically produced goods which do not bear the tariff and often to raise budgetary revenue. In the specific case of the UK, there is no domestic tobacco manufacturing company (and related jobs) to protect. In light of the current state of the UK tobacco manufacturing industry and the overall tobacco tax structure, it indeed seems unnecessary to resort to tariffs unless the UK Government decides to use import tariffs to raise additional revenues or as bargaining chip in future negotiations with the EU. The indirect impact of tariffs on illicit tobacco trade could mainly result from higher retail prices pushing consumers of licit products toward the illicit market.

All in all however, import tariffs are not expected to play a significant role under most Brexit scenarios. Indeed, if the UK remains in the single market or in the customs union (first and second scenarios, respectively) it would continue to grant duty free access to products that originate from the EU Member States. The same can be assumed in case the EU and the UK negotiate a trade agreement (third scenario) based on the precedents set by existing FTAs. '*Hard Brexit*' is the only scenario where one could envisage tariffs being effectively levied on imports of licit tobacco products from the EU entering into the UK market. Conversely, one could argue that import tariffs could be lowered for all imports (EU and non-EU countries) in case of a '*Hard Brexit*' where the UK would enjoy full freedom in the realm of trade regulation. This could contribute to lowering the retail price of tobacco products (even if only

---

[37] See Webb (2019) UK progress in rolling over EU trade agreements.

[38] See HM Government (2019b) Guidance—The Customs Tariff (Preferential Trade Agreement) (EU Exit) Regulations 2019. This sets out the individual product duty rates and preferential rules of origin that will apply because of preferential agreements made between the UK and third countries, including Free Trade Agreements.

[39] TMA (2017) TMA response to HMG's white paper on Customs.

[40] Ibid. In its note, TMA also concluded that the introduction of tariff barriers would only serve to complicate the current tobacco excise regime.

[41] HM Revenue and Customs (2019b) 2018–19 Annual Report and Accounts, p. 179.

marginally given that excise is usually a more impactful pricing instrument), thus encouraging illicit consumers to move to licit sources.

4.1.3 Tobacco Regulations

Beside taxation (including the EMCS) and trade discussed above, the legal framework related to illicit trade in tobacco products includes the regulation of tobacco manufacturers, the licensing of wholesale and retail sellers, the regulation of raw tobacco, tobacco machinery licensing, as well as a number of requirements resulting from the EU Tobacco Products Directive. The latter are analysed in a separate section. The purpose of these instruments is to support tobacco control policies and protect the national budget by preventing tax evasion through illicit trade.

Regulation of Tobacco Manufacturers
Although tobacco manufacturing has ceased in the UK, tobacco manufacturers who supply the UK market must comply with the full range of relevant legislation, including tobacco product regulations, as set out in the *Standardised Packaging of Tobacco Products Regulations 2015* and the *Tobacco and Related Products Regulations 2016*. Both pieces of legislation implement *EU Directive 2014/40*.[42]

Regulation of Raw Tobacco
Controlling raw tobacco supplies limits the risk of illegal manufacture of tobacco products and consequent duty evasion either through processing into smoking products in unregistered premises, or selling in small quantities to consumers for home processing. Tobacco is not grown in the UK. Also, contrary to tobacco products, raw tobacco is not subject to excise duty. In 2018, the EU Commission concluded that including raw tobacco in the scope of excisable goods is not justified and the

---

[42]The *Standardised Packaging of Tobacco Products Regulations* 2015 implement Articles 13 and 14, and one element of Article 9.3 of *EU Directive 2014/40*. The *Tobacco and Related Products Regulations 2016* implement *EU Directive 2014/40* other than Articles 6, 13–16, one element of Article 9.3, and certain aspects of Article 20.5, as well as *Commission Delegated Directive 2014/109/EU of 10 October 2014 amending Annex II to Directive 2014/40/EU of the European Parliament and of the Council by establishing the library of picture warnings to be used on tobacco products*; *Commission Implementing Decision (EU) 2015/1735 of 24 September 2015 on the precise position of the general warning and the information message on roll-your-own tobacco marketed in pouches*; *Commission Implementing Decision (EU) 2015/1842 of 9 October 2015 on the technical specifications for the layout, design and shape of the combined health warnings for tobacco products for smoking*; *Commission Implementing Decision (EU) 2015/2183 of 24 November 2015 establishing a common format for the notification of electronic cigarettes and refill containers*; *Commission Implementing Decision (EU) 2015/2186 of 25 November 2015 establishing a format for the submission and making available of information on tobacco products*; *Commission Implementing Decision (EU) 2016/586 of 14 April 2016 on technical standards for the refill mechanism of electronic cigarettes*; and *Directive 2001/31/EC of the European Parliament and Council of 8 June 2000 on certain legal aspects of information society service, in particular electronic commerce, in the Internal Market* (the 'E-commerce Directive') in relation to electronic cigarette advertising.

administrative costs of such a measure would be disproportionate to its foreseeable benefits.[43]

Pursuant to the *Raw Tobacco (Approval Scheme) Regulations 2016*, businesses and individuals are prohibited from carrying on any activity involving raw tobacco unless they have obtained approval from HMRC. The scheme has been introduced to prevent the illegal manufacture of tobacco products, reduce the risk of excise duty evasion, and control the movement of raw tobacco in the UK.[44]

Tobacco Machinery Licensing

Since April 2018, a registration scheme has been in operation to license manufacturing machinery used to make tobacco products in the UK, as set out in the *Tobacco Products Manufacturing Machinery (Licensing Scheme) Regulations 2018*.[45] Under the licensing scheme, anybody manufacturing, purchasing, acquiring, owning, or in possession of tobacco-manufacturing machinery must hold a license issued by HMRC. HMRC assesses the 'fit and proper' status of the applicants and their proposed use of the machine prior to issue of a licence.

Although HMRC expects the scheme to have very few users, it gives HMRC additional powers to tackle the evasion of excise duty on tobacco products through the control of tobacco product manufacturing machinery and thus to tackle the illegal manufacturing of tobacco products.[46] The introduction of penalties and forfeitures of manufacturing machinery in case of non-compliance, as foreseen under Part 5 of the Regulations, offers a stronger disincentive than the simple payment of a fine. The measure can help prevent the diversion of tobacco-producing machinery into the illicit market, or at least make such diversion more difficult, thus facilitating law enforcement. Notably, the licensing scheme introduced in 2018 implements Article

---

[43] European Commission (2018c) Report from the Commission to the Council on Directive 2011/64/EU on the structure and rates of excise duty applied to manufactured tobacco, p. 4. In its analysis, the EU Commission found that there are other means to control raw tobacco, for instance the requirement that economic operators register and keep records of stocks and flows of raw tobacco, as it is already the case in several Member States, including the UK.

[44] HM Revenue and Customs (2016) Excise Notice 2003: Tobacco Duty—the Raw Tobacco Approval Scheme.

[45] HMRC has also published Excise Notice 2004: Tobacco Duty—Tobacco Products Manufacturing Machine Licensing Scheme.

[46] Pursuant to Article 3 (1) "*A person may not carry out a regulated activity otherwise than in accordance with a licence granted by the Commissioners under these Regulations*". Article 4 describes a 'regulated activity' as the manufacture, purchase, acquisition, ownership or possession of an item of tobacco products manufacturing machinery. Tobacco products manufacturing machinery has the meaning given in section 8V(1) of the Tobacco Products Duty Act 1979. Further, Part 3 of the Regulations provides that the Commissioners can only grant a licence if they are satisfied that the applicant is a fit and proper person and will not use the machinery for the fraudulent evasion of duty charged on tobacco products; may prescribe in a notice, and specify in a licence, conditions and restrictions to which a licence is subject; and may vary or revoke a licence at any time for reasonable cause.

6 of the *WHO FCTC Protocol to eliminate illicit trade in tobacco products* (ITP) on 'Licence, equivalent approval or control system'.[47] ITP Article 6 para. 1 states:

> [...] each Party shall prohibit the conduct of any of the following activities by any natural or legal person except pursuant to a licence or equivalent approval (hereafter "licence") granted, or control system implemented, by a competent authority in accordance with national law: (a) manufacture of tobacco products and manufacturing equipment; and (b) import or export of tobacco products and manufacturing equipment.[48]

Internet and Overseas (Distance) Sales

In the UK, buying tobacco products over the internet from another EU country for personal use is permitted. TPD-2 gives Member States two options in relation to cross-border distance sales to consumers—either to prohibit such sales or to require sellers to register with the competent authorities in Member States where actual or potential customers are located.[49] So far, a minority of EU Member States (e.g. France and Finland) have chosen to ban these sale, thus preventing consumers from ordering tobacco products from abroad.[50]

TPD-2, adopted in 2014, introduces common rules on the registration of retail outlets engaging in such sales. The UK implemented this requirement through Article 47 of the *UK Tobacco and Related Products Regulations of 2016* prescribing that all retail outlets intending to engage in cross-border distance sales shall submit a comprehensive set of information to the Secretary of State, including name or corporate name and permanent address of the place of activity from where the tobacco products will be supplied, the starting date of the activity of offering tobacco products for cross-border distance sales to consumers, and the address of the website or websites used for that purpose and all relevant information necessary to identify the website. In the UK, sellers are required to register by completing a form which is submitted to HMRC, charge customers the relevant amount of tax, and make arrangements for

---

[47] See HM Revenue and Customs (2018b) Tobacco Duty: Illicit Trade Protocol—licensing of tobacco manufacturing machinery.

[48] FCTC Article 6 falls into Part III 'Supply Chain Control'. Art. 6 para. 2 further requires *"Each Party shall endeavour to license, to the extent considered appropriate, and when the following activities are not prohibited by national law, any natural or legal person engaged in: (a) retailing of tobacco products; (b) growing of tobacco, except for traditional small-scale growers, farmers and producers; (c) transporting commercial quantities of tobacco products or manufacturing equipment; and (d) wholesaling, brokering, warehousing or distribution of tobacco and tobacco products or manufacturing equipment"*.

[49] TPD-2 Art. 18. TPD-2 Rec. 33 nevertheless acknowledge how *"Cross-border distance sales of tobacco products could facilitate access to tobacco products that do not comply with this Directive. There is also an increased risk that young people would get access to tobacco products. Consequently, there is a risk that tobacco control legislation would be undermined."*.

[50] Some EU countries have yet to determine their position on this issue. Information on the regime applicable in the various EU/EEA Member States is available at Public Health England (2020b) Member states that permit cross-border distance sales of tobacco and e-cigarette products.

these taxes to be paid.[51] The list of registered tobacco products retailers is published by Public Health England.[52]

There have been calls for the introduction of a ban on cross-border distance sales to consumers in the UK.[53] Considering the flexibility already provided by EU law on this matter, Brexit is unlikely to have any direct effect on the approach chosen by the UK, regardless of the final form of Brexit.

The impact of Brexit on these regulatory measures can be summarized as follows. '*Soft Brexit*', where the UK remains in the single market, is the scenario that would provide the highest possible regulatory stability. The EU legislation on which some of the regulations above is based, i.e. *EU Directive 2014/40*, represent legal norms applicable to EEA. The situation would change if the UK remains in the customs union leaving however the single market. In both instances, changes to the current regulatory regime would not be automatic and are more theoretical in the absence of continous efforts and enormous resource. This topic may also not feature highly on the regulatory agenda of the regulator in the complicated post-Brexit scenario. The same need for legislative efforts and resource applies in case of a freetrade agreement or the '*Hard Brexit*' scenarios. Finally, Brexit would have no impact on obligations resulting from the ITP, such as the licensing scheme introduced in 2018. As a party to the ITP in its own right, the UK will continue to be bound by this international instrument after Brexit.

4.2 The Enforcement Framework

Beside an effective legal framework, robust investigation and enforcement mechanisms are indispensable to counter illicit trade in tobacco products. In the UK, this task is left to a number of different actors that operate at the local, national, and international levels. The UK being a target market for illicit tobacco products, international cooperation plays an important role in detecting and disrupting international networks and tackling the problem in source and transit countries alike. The UK's approach to disrupting the illicit supply chain can be described as 'end-to-end', requiring action both inland and overseas. Illicit tobacco products sold on the UK market are mainly imported from other EU Member States and often the latter are transit countries, with the products originating outside of the EU. Close collaboration with EU and Member States' agencies is therefore of paramount importance under all Brexit scenarios.

---

[51] Public Health England (2016) Tobacco products and e-cigarette cross-border sales registration.
[52] Public Health England (2020a) List of registered retailers.
[53] ASH (2019) The Tobacco Products (Traceability and Security Features) Regulations 2019, Consultation response on behalf of ASH on the draft secondary legislation.

4.2.1 UK Institutions

At the national level, the two principal actors in the fight against illicit tobacco trade are HMRC[54] and UK Border Force[55] (previously Border Agency). Since 2008, they share responsibility for tackling illicit tobacco trade in the UK, for developing intelligence, and reducing revenue losses (budget protection). Despite the many synergies, they have fundamentally distinct roles. HMRC has responsibility for collecting and enforcing tobacco duties, investigating and disrupting criminal offences, and detecting and disrupting the supply of illicit tobacco inland.[56] The UK Border Force, a law enforcement command within the Home Office, undertakes enforcement work at the border for HMRC. It is in charge of detecting and seizing smuggled tobacco at the border, arresting those suspected of smuggling and referring them to HMRC for investigation.[57]

Various institutions play different investigative and enforcement roles, including the National Crime Agency (NCA), UK's lead agency against organised crime and the UK point of contact for foreign agencies such as Interpol, Europol and other international law enforcement agencies, and the British Police. At the local level, the Trading Standards promote and enforce fair, safe, and legal trading practices. Covering a wide range of consumer protection activites, they are responsible for developing local intelligence and detecting and seizing illicit tobacco products.[58] Trading Standards play an important role in tackling illicit tobacco trade, including through social media and online platforms—see for instance their involvement in *Operation Jasper*.[59] Other important national actors include the Market Surveillance Authorities and the Intellectual Property Office of the United Kingdom (UKIPO), particularly with regard to counterfeit tobacco products.[60]

International investigative functions are mainly carried out through the HMRC's network of *Fiscal Crime Liaison Officers* (FCLOs). FCLOs are responsible for liaising with international fiscal and law-enforcement agencies and developing intelligence to intercept illicit tobacco destined for the UK market. The FCLO network consists of officers located in countries stretching across Europe to the Far East.

---

[54] https://www.gov.uk/government/organisations/hm-revenue-customs.
[55] https://www.gov.uk/government/organisations/border-force.
[56] https://www.gov.uk/government/organisations/hm-revenue-customs.
[57] https://www.gov.uk/government/organisations/border-force.
[58] http://www.nationaltradingstandards.uk/what-we-do/.
[59] See for instance CTSI (2019) Collaboration brings down illegal tobacco operations.
[60] Tobacco remains among the most investigated IP crime sectors in the UK. The IPO, as part of the government's Serious and Organised Crime strategy, does significant amounts of work to reduce the level of illegal content online. This includes tackling trade in counterfeit goods, increasing education and awareness, and building respect for intellectual property. The IPO itself also works closely with HMRC and its enforcement team has identified cases which have already provided opportunities to disrupt Organised Crime Groups through taxation. See, for instance, UK-IPO (2018) *IP Crime and Enforcement Report 2017–2018*.

Brexit could encourage increased coordination among the various actors in the UK. Such efforts could go beyond tobacco and be structured across sectors, involving other counterfeit goods such as electronic equipment, clothing and footwear, toys and games, and leather goods. For instance, in 2018, the *Illicit Trade All Party Parliamentary Group* (APPG) proposed the creation of a UK *Anti-Illicit Trade Group* (AITG). Partners of the AITG could include regional policing units, HMRC, Treasury, Border Force, National Trading Standards, consumer advisory groups, trade associations, and businesses. Among AITG's main tasks would be to function as a forum for partnership, coordination through dialogue, information, intelligence sharing and strengthening cross-organizational relationships, as well as to facilitate the development of a comprehensive UK national anti-illicit trade strategy.[61]

4.2.2 Current Collaboration with EU Agencies and Bodies

As an EU Member State, the UK was an active participant in the work of the different European agencies which tackle illicit tobacco trade and, more generally, participated in EU police and judicial cooperation in criminal matters, including in the context of information exchange databases and systems.

The fight against illicit tobacco trade in the EU is conducted with a combination of strong legislative responses, robust law enforcement and enhanced cooperation at national, European, and international levels. In particular, OLAF, Europol, Frontex, and Eurojust contribute to strengthening enforcement, detection, and sanctions, and to enhancing cooperation and coordination in analysis and intelligence.

Deriving its jurisdiction from the budget offence element of illicit tobacco trade, OLAF plays a central role in tackling illicit tobacco trade and has an explicit mandate to fight cigarette smuggling as part of the EU efforts to curb this phenomenon.[62] In 2017, OLAF seized a total of approximately 470 million cigarettes, equal to an estimated loss to public budgets of €94 million.[63] OLAF works in close cooperation with national law enforcement agencies and customs services both inside and outside of the EU to prevent, detect, and investigate tobacco smuggling, so that evaded duties can be recovered and perpetrators prosecuted.

HMRC works closely with OLAF, collaborating at strategic level by sharing information and analysing risks, and has initiated and delivered joint operations with other Member States funded by OLAF. For instance, '*Joint Customs Operation (JCO) Magnum II*' targeted the smuggling of tobacco products transported by road into the EU territory from third countries such as Belarus, Ukraine, and Russia. The operation,

---

[61] APPG (2018) Illicit Trade in the UK.

[62] OLAF is not and EU agency, it is part of the EU Commission. Currently, OLAF has four directorates, two of which deal with investigations, one with investigation support and one with policy. The staff is about 420 members. OLAF's organigram is available here https://ec.europa.eu/anti-fraud/sites/antifraud/files/orgchart_en.pdf.

[63] Ilett (2018) The Illicit Tobacco Trade—What do we Know?

which was coordinated by the Estonian Customs Administration and OLAF with the involvement of fourteen Member States—including the UK—as well as Europol and Frontex, led to the seizure of roughly 20 million cigarettes.[64] OLAF is also tracking the movements of suspicious containers, in cooperation with the competent services of the Member States and third countries, as well as with international organisations, to avoid the diversion of cigarettes onto the EU contraband market. Combating tobacco smuggling is among the main activities of *Hercule III*, an anti-fraud program implemented by OLAF with a total budget of €104.9 million.[65]

The *European Union Agency for Law Enforcement Cooperation*, or Europol, is the law enforcement agency of the EU formed in 1998 to handle criminal intelligence and combat serious international organised crime and terrorism through cooperation between the competent authorities of EU Member States. Excise fraud remains among the priorities for the fight against organised and serious international crime.[66] Since 2010, Europol has promoted EMPACT *(European Multidisciplinary Platform against Criminal Threats)* projects, several of which specifically relate to illicit trade in tobacco products, for instance aiming at disrupting smuggling in shipping containers. With a permanently seconded officer at Europol, HMRC engages with pan-European intelligence and analysis on tobacco fraud, and support projects driven by Europol.

The unlawful manufacturing and smuggling of excise goods, including tobacco and cigarettes, is also among Europol's Analysis Projects, under which specialists support EU law enforcement authorities and other partner organisations to tackle organised crime.[67] For instance, operation 'TSAR', coordinated by Europol in collaboration with Eurojust, resulted in the break up a large network of counterfeit cigarette smugglers operating from Ukraine to the United Kingdom.[68]

Frontex, the European Border and Coast Guard Agency, carries out operational activities focusing on cigarette smuggling across the EU-Eastern land border, a major source of illicit tobacco products. Frontex efforts have led to important seizures of

---

[64]OLAF (2018) The OLAF Report 2017.

[65]See *Regulation (EU) No 250/2014 of the European Parliament and of the Council of 26 February 2014 establishing a programme to promote activities in the field of the protection of the financial interests of the European Union (Hercule III programme) and repealing Decision No 804/2004/EC*. With a total budget of €104.9 million, the program for instance finances the purchase by national authorities of investigation tools to carry out analyses of samples taken from cigarettes and tobacco seizures and determine whether seized cigarettes are genuine or counterfeit, of x-ray scanners in harbours and airports and computers for automated number plate recognition systems or to build the storage of seized cigarettes and tobacco awaiting for destruction. In the context of the new multiannual financial framework (2021–2027) the EU Commission has adopted a proposal for a new EU Anti-Fraud Programme, which essentially builds on the Hercule III programme and combine it with other activities that OLAF already performs. See European Commission (2018b) EU budget: €181 million to strengthen the fight against fraud affecting the EU budget.

[66]Council of the EU (2017) Council conclusions on setting the EU's priorities for the fight against organised and serious international crime between 2018 and 2021.

[67]Europol Analysis Projects. https://www.europol.europa.eu/crime-areas-trends/europol-analysis-projects.

[68]Europol (2011) Large International Operation Against Cigarette Smuggling Networks.

illicit tobacco products and to the breaking up of organised cross-border crime at the EU's borders with Western Balkan countries, Southeast Europe, and select border crossing points at the Eastern land border.[69] As a target market for illicit tobacco products, the UK benefits from this type of operations.

Judicial cooperation in criminal matters is another important field in the fight against illicit trade in tobacco products. Eurojust was set up in 2002 to *"support and strengthen coordination and cooperation between national investigating and prosecuting authorities in relation to serious crime [...]"*, as outlined in Article 85 of the TFEU *(Treaty on the Functioning of the European Union)*.[70] One of the key instruments by which Eurojust supports and strengthens coordination and cooperation is through the facilitation and funding of joint investigation teams, which play a crucial role in combating cross-border serious and organised crime. Crime groups are often active in illicit tobacco trade, among other activities.[71]

As EU Member State, the UK also participated in the *Customs Cooperation Working Party* (CCWP) of the European Council.[72] The CCWP handles work regarding operational cooperation among national customs administrations with a view to increasing their enforcement capabilities. It also defines strategic and tactical objectives for Joint Customs Operations. The CCWP focuses on seeking results in terms of seizures, identification of new threats, and disruption of criminal gangs by cooperating closely with Europol, Eurojust, and OLAF. Illicit tobacco trade is a recurrent topic on the CCWP agenda.

Continued participation in the work of EU agencies and bodies fighting illicit tobacco trade is important considering the UK's geographic location, the fact that it is a target market, and that EU Member States are either origin or transit countries for illicit products sold on the UK market. The many successes achieved so far corroborate this view.

It should be noted that third-country participation in EU agencies and bodies is not new. For instance, the EFTA states (Iceland, Liechtenstein, Norway, and Switzerland) participate extensively in the work of EU agencies. Generally, they do not have voting rights in the agencies' decision-making fora and may have to contribute to agency budgets. Participation in EU agencies is also part of the EU's Enlargement Strategy, according to which agencies are encouraged to offer participation possibilities, including observer status, to candidate countries in Management Board and

---

[69] See, for instance, Frontex (2018) 23 smugglers arrested, drugs and cigarettes seized during Frontex-led operation.

[70] Article 3 of the *Council Decision of 28 February 2002 setting up Eurojust with a view to reinforcing the fight against serious crime* states that the objectives of Eurojust shall be to support the competent authorities of the Member States to render their investigations and prosecutions more effective, and to improve cooperation between the competent authorities of the Member States.

[71] See, for instance, Europol (2019) Operational Task Force Leads to Dismantling of One of Europe's Most Prolific Crime Groups Behind €680 million operation.

[72] See https://www.consilium.europa.eu/en/council-eu/preparatory-bodies/customs-cooperation-working-party/.

expert group meetings.[73] Collaboration is in the interest of both sides. After all, the UK will be leaving the EU but not Europe. The examples provided above suggest that the EU can accommodate different scenarios. As much in the same way as other aspects analysed in this project, the future cooperation among EU and UK agencies is likely to be commensurate with the scope and depth of the future relationship.

4.2.3 Possible Forms of Post-Brexit Cooperation with EU Agencies

In order to efficiently control illicit trade in tobacco, close post-Brexit collaboration seems to be in the interest of both the UK and the EU. The *2019 Withdrawal Agreement* only regulates the question of the transition period, for instance by stating at Art. 131 that:

> During the transition period, the institutions, bodies, offices and agencies of the Union shall have the powers conferred upon them by Union law in relation to the United Kingdom and to natural and legal persons residing or established in the United Kingdom. In particular, the Court of Justice of the European Union (ECJ) shall have jurisdiction as provided for in the Treaties.

The 2019 Political Declaration contains references to cooperation, including in "law enforcement and judicial cooperation in criminal matters, foreign policy, security and defence, as well as thematic cooperation in areas of common interest".[74] The 2018 Withdrawal Act does not provide more guidance and only states at para. 19 ('Future interaction with [...] agencies of the EU') that "nothing in this Act shall prevent the United Kingdom from [...] (b) continuing to participate in, or have a formal relationship with, the agencies of the EU after exit day".

Some guidance can be found in the founding acts of the EU agencies described above, as they set out the modalities of participation, budgetary contribution, and staffing arrangements which can be made by third states. For instance, the *Decision*

---

[73] The EU Instrument for Pre-Accession Assistance (European Commission (2020b) Overview—Instrument for Pre-Accession Assistance), provides funding to EU agencies to help prepare candidate states for participation in certain agencies. TEU Article 8 provides that the EU *"shall develop a special relationship with neighbouring countries, aiming to establish an area of prosperity and good neighbourliness, founded on the values of the Union and characterised by close and peaceful relations based on cooperation"*. Article 8 also provides that the EU *"may conclude specific agreements" with ENP countries, which "may contain reciprocal rights and obligations as well as the possibility of undertaking activities jointly"*.

[74] 2019 Political Declaration, recital 81.

of the EU Council establishing Europol provides at Article 23 para. 1 ('Relations with third States and organisations') that "[...] Europol may [] establish and maintain cooperative relations with: (a) third States".[75] Today, Europol has such arrangements with administrations in several third countries.[76]

There are two types of cooperation agreements that Europol can enter into with states and other entities outside of the EU—strategic agreements and operational agreements. While both types of agreements are aimed at enhancing cooperation between Europol and the country concerned, there is one major difference. Strategic agreements are limited to the exchange of general intelligence as well as strategic and technical information, whereas operational agreements allow for the exchange of information, including personal data.[77] The system of liaison officers at Europol ensures that the interests of law enforcement agencies in the EU Member States and non-EU partners are represented in Europol's headquarters.

As a non-EU Member, the UK would foreseeably not be able to continue interacting with the Europol through its designated Europol National Unit (ENU).[78] Rather, upon conclusion of an arrangement, ideally an operational agreement, the UK, like other non-EU countries, would have a liaison officer. Today, liaison officers from non-EU countries include European non-EU countries (e.g. Iceland, Norway, Switzerland), and a handful of countries from different continents (e.g. Australia, Canada, Colombia). Liaison officers from several United States law enforcement agencies are also hosted at Europol.

Likewise, Frontex cooperates and collaborates with third countries at a technical and operational level on the basis of status agreements or other bilateral agreements. The terms of cooperation are set out in Article 54 ('Cooperation with third countries') of *Regulation 2016/1624*,[79] where para. 7 foresees that *"The Agency may, with the agreement of the Member States concerned, invite observers from third countries to participate in its activities at the external borders."* Frontex has concluded working arrangements with the authorities of 18 countries: *the Russian Federation, Ukraine, Moldova, Georgia, the former Yugoslav Republic of Macedonia, Serbia, Albania, Bosnia and Herzegovina, the United States, Montenegro, Belarus, Canada, Cape*

---

[75] Council Decision 2009/371/JHA of 6 April 2009 establishing the European Police Office (Europol).

[76] See Europol (2020) Partners and Agreements.

[77] See also *Council Decision 2009/935/JHA of 30 November 2009 determining the list of third States and organisations with which Europol shall conclude agreements*. In addition, *Council Decision 2009/934/JHA of November 2009* contains implementing rules governing Europol's relations with partners, including the exchange of personal data and classified information. Under Article 4, agreements can only be concluded once the Council has decided, after consulting the European Parliament.

[78] Each ENU seconds at least one representative to Europol headquarters, where every Member State is provided with its own office.

[79] Regulation (EU) 2016/1624 of the European Parliament and of the Council of 14 September 2016 on the European Border and Coast Guard and amending Regulation (EU) 2016/399 of the European Parliament and of the Council and repealing Regulation (EC) No 863/2007 of the European Parliament and of the Council, Council Regulation (EC) No 2007/2004 and Council Decision 2005/267/EC.

4.2 The Enforcement Framework

Verde, Nigeria, Armenia, Turkey, Azerbaijan and Kosovo, as well as with the *CIS Border Troop Commanders Council* and the *MARRI Regional Centre in the Western Balkans*.[80] Eurojust is also open to cooperation with third countries, as provided for in the Agency's founding act, which devotes Section III to 'International cooperation' (Article 52).[81]

Regarding OLAF, Art. 93 of the *2019 Withdrawal Agreement* establishes a transitional period (*'New State aid and European Anti-Fraud Office procedures'*) during which it remains competent to initiate new investigations regarding facts that occurred before the end of the Brexit transition period (now set for 31 December 2020 pursuant to Art. 126 of the *2019 Withdrawal Agreement*). In a scenario where the UK remains in the customs union, OLAF may also play a role in the future and if the two parties agree on 'common procedures and processes' for the collection of VAT on trade between the UK and the EU, to avoid the need for fiscal border controls on goods moving in either direction. Since customs duties and the VAT base are an EU 'own resource' affecting the revenue side of its budget, any such arrangement could require UK authorities to work with OLAF (since it investigates irregularities affecting the EU budget).[82] The exact parameters of such cooperation would be a matter for negotiation.

Also relevant to the enforcement of anti-illicit tobacco actions, is the *European Arrest Warrant* system. Established in 2002, the system allows EU members to request the arrest and detention of criminals in other countries without extradition talks between them. According to the National Crime Agency, other EU Members requested the arrest of 14,279 UK-based suspects in 2015–16, up from 1865 in 2004. The UK made 241 such requests in 2015–16, leading to 150 arrests. Title V of the Withdrawal Agreement (*'Ongoing judicial cooperation proceedings in criminal matters'*) provides for a transitional period including in respect of European arrest warrants where the requested person was arrested before the end of the transition period for the purposes of the execution of a European arrest warrant.[83] After Brexit however, it could prove difficult for the UK to remain part of the system as a result of the UK opting out from the free movement rules and largely ending the jurisdiction of the European Court of Justice. Instead, a streamlined extradition process could be

---

[80] The working arrangements can be consulted online through the Frontex database at https://frontex.europa.eu/about-frontex/key-documents/?category=working-arrangements-with-non-eu-countries. Generally, working arrangements concluded by Frontex include a statement that they do not constitute an international agreement and do not fulfil international obligations of the EU.

[81] Regulation (EU) 2018/1727 of the European Parliament and of the Council of 14 November 2018 on the European Union Agency for Criminal Justice Cooperation (Eurojust).

[82] See UK Parliament (2019) Background and Committee's conclusions on Proposal for a Regulation amending Regulation 883/2013. Also, although not directly relevant for the issue of illicit tobacco trade, if the UK remains a participant in a number of EU funding programmes as a 'third country' (such as the Framework Programme for Research and the Euratom nuclear research programme), is likely to require acceptance of OLAF's jurisdiction to investigate potential irregularities with EU funding in the UK.

[83] Article 62 Paragraph 1(b).

considered.[84] The same difficulties are likely to emerge with regard to the *European Criminal Records Information System* (ECRIS), where there is no precedent of access to the system granted to a third country.

It remains to be seen whether the existing forms of collaboration with third countries are adequate to the UK's unique situation. Some have expressed concerns about the diminished ability to influence work in key EU agencies.[85] The most adequate solution would also take into account the availability of alternative fora already providing a framework for cooperation between the EU and the UK beyond that of the EU, such as the Council of Europe or Lyon-based Interpol, the world's largest international police organisation that takes part in the fight against illicit trade in tobacco products in Europe and on a global level by facilitating international police cooperation. However, a paper prepared by the EU Parliament in 2018 suggests that simply relying on existing alternative frameworks would result in a *"substantial reduction in the level of cooperation when compared to the current situation, including a reduction in the level of intelligence available to the EU [and to the UK]"*.[86]

Finally, two international organizations of great importance in the fight against illicit trade in tobacco products are the Brussels-based *World Customs Organization* (WCO) and the *World Health Organization* (WHO) based in Geneva. The WCO has quasi-universal membership and represents 183 customs administrations across the globe that collectively process approximately 98% of world trade. The UK has been a member since 1952. While the WCO does not by itself actively fight illicit tobacco trade, it provides a valuable venue for discussions among customs authorities worldwide, for analysing and sharing best practices, and for collecting and disseminating data. For instance, since 2012 the WCO publishes the annual *Illicit Trade Report* which contributes to the study of the phenomenon of illicit trade through the analysis of seizure data and case studies—including on tobacco products—voluntarily submitted by Member Customs administrations from around the globe to the WCO through the Customs Enforcement Network (CEN) database.[87]

The WHO, a quasi-universal specialized agency of the United Nations with 194 Members, including the UK, deals with illicit trade in tobacco products since such activity can undermine tobacco policies aimed at reducing the harmful effects of tobacco. In 2003, WHO Member States unanimously adopted the *WHO Framework Convention on Tobacco Control* (WHO FCTC), the only public health treaty under

---

[84] See, for instance, BBC (2018) UK can't keep European Arrest Warrant after Brexit, reporting the views expressed by EU Chief Negotiator Michel Barnier. Also see Policy Department for Citizens' Rights and Constitutional Affairs (2018).

[85] See, for instance, the statement by Alex Rothwell, City of London Police, *"From a policing perspective, our relationship with Europol is critical. Sharing intelligence and developing practical opportunities to counter crime are key benefits. It is anticipated that if the UK is no longer a member of the European Union whilst we will continue to contribute to Europol, our ability to influence activity will be diminished."*—APPG (2018) p. 13.

[86] Policy Department for Citizens' Rights and Constitutional Affairs (2018), p. 9.

[87] Between 2008 and 2011 WCO published an annual 'Customs and Tobacco Report'. Since 2012 the publication has been untied into the Illicit Trade Report, WCO's flagship publication. http://www.wcoomd.org/en/topics/enforcement-and-compliance/resources/publications.aspx.

the auspices of WHO. More recently, Parties to the FCTC negotiated the *Protocol to Eliminate Illicit Trade in Tobacco Products* (ITP), an international treaty with the objective of eliminating all forms of illicit trade in tobacco products through a package of measures to be taken by countries acting in cooperation with each other. The ITP is discussed further in Sect. 6.2 below.

The UK's standalone membership in relevant international organizations, such as the WCO and the WHO, and international treaty-based initiatives such as the FCTC and the ITP, will continue after Brexit without the need for re-negotiations with the rest of the membership, as it is for instance the case for the UK's participation in the World Trade Organization (WTO).

References

APPG (2018) Illicit trade in the UK. Illicit Trade All Party Parliamentary Group (APPG), July 2018. https://connectpa.co.uk/wp-content/uploads/2018/07/Illicit-Trade-APPG-report-2018LRi.pdf. Accessed 24 Feb 2020

ASH (2019) The tobacco products (traceability and security features) regulations 2019, Consultation response on behalf of ASH on the draft secondary legislation. http://ash.org.uk/wp-content/uploads/2019/03/ASH_conrresponse_TPtraceabilitySecurity2019FINAL.pdf. Accessed 24 Feb 2020

Bate R, Kallen C, Mathur A (2019) The perverse effect of sin taxes: the rise of illicit white cigarettes. Appl Econ 52(8):789–805

BBC (2018) UK can't keep European Arrest Warrant after Brexit. BBC Online, 19 June 2018. https://www.bbc.com/news/uk-politics-44532500. Accessed 24 Feb 2020

Calder S (2019) Holidays after Brexit: Everything you need to know about customs and duty free. The Independent, 1 Mar 2019. https://www.independent.co.uk/travel/news-and-advice/brexit-customs-explained-duty-free-travel-uk-eu-a8802901.html. Accessed 24 Feb 2020

Council conclusions on setting the EU's priorities for the fight against organised and serious international crime between 2018 and 2021. Council of the European Union, Brussels, May 2017. http://data.consilium.europa.eu/doc/document/ST-8654-2017-INIT/en/pdf. Accessed 24 Feb 2020

Council Decision 2009/371/JHA of 6 April 2009 establishing the European Police Office (Europol). OJ L 121/37

Council Decision 2009/935/JHA of 30 November 2009 determining the list of third States and organisations with which Europol shall conclude agreements. OJ L 325/12 11.12.2009, pp 12–13

Council Decision of 28 February 2002 setting up Eurojust with a view to reinforcing the fight against serious crime. OJ L 063, 06/03/2002, pp 01–13

Council Directive 2006/112/EC of 28 November 2006 on the common system of value added tax, OJ L 347, 11.12.2006, pp 1–118

Council Directive 2007/74/EC of 20 December 2007 on the exemption from value added tax and excise duty of goods imported by persons travelling from third countries. OJ L 346, 29.12.2007, pp 6–12

Council Directive 2008/118/EC of 16 December 2008 concerning the general arrangements for excise duty and repealing Directive 92/12/EEC. OJ L 9, 14.1.2009, pp 12–30

Council Directive 2010/88/EU of 7 December 2010 amending Directive 2006/112/EC on the common system of value added tax, with regard to the duration of the obligation to respect a minimum standard rate, OJ L 326, 10.12.2010, pp 1–2

Council Directive 2011/64/EU of 21 June 2011 on the structure and rates of excise duty applied to manufactured tobacco, OJ L 176, 5.7.2011, pp 24–36

Council of EU (2009) Council Decision 2009/934/JHA of November 2009 contains implementing rules governing Europol's relations with partners, including the exchange of personal data and classified information. OJ L 325, 11.12.2009, pp 6–11

CTSI (2019) Collaboration brings down illegal tobacco operations. Chartered Trading Standards Institute, 28 Jan 2019. https://www.tradingstandards.uk/news-policy/news-room/2019/collaboration-brings-down-illegal-tobacco-operations. Accessed 24 Feb 2020

Dathan M (2019) Return of the booze cruise—brits to get duty free back on alcohol and tobacco for trips to Europe under No Deal Brexit. The Sun, 4 Mar 2019. https://www.thesun.co.uk/news/brexit/8561345/duty-free-return-alcohol-tobacco-no-deal-brexit/. Accessed 24 Feb 2020

Directive 2014/40/EU of the European Parliament and of the Council of 3 April 2014 on the approximation of the laws, regulations and administrative provisions of the Member States concerning the manufacture, presentation and sale of tobacco and related products and repealing Directive 2001/37/EC, OJ L 127, 29.4.2014

Elliott L (2019) Duty-free purchases of cigarettes and alcohol to return under no-deal Brexit. The Guardian, 10 Sept 2019. https://www.theguardian.com/politics/2019/sep/10/duty-free-purchases-of-cigarettes-and-alcohol-to-return-under-no-deal-brexit. Accessed 24 Feb 2020

European Commission (2018a) Annex to the Communication from the Commission to the European Parliament, the Council and the European Economic and Social Committee 2nd Action Plan to fight the illicit tobacco trade 2018–2022. European Commission, 7.12.2018 COM(2018) 846 final

European Commission (2018b) EU budget: €181 million to strengthen the fight against fraud affecting the EU budget. European Commission, 30 May 2018. https://europa.eu/rapid/press-release_IP-18-3967_en.htm. Accessed 24 Feb 2020

European Commission (2018c) Report from the Commission to the Council on Directive 2011/64/EU on the structure and rates of excise duty applied to manufactured tobacco. Brussels, 12.01.2018 COM(2018) 17 final. https://eur-lex.europa.eu/legal-content/EN/TXT/HTML/?uri=CELEX:52018DC0017&from=EN. Accessed 24 Feb 2020

European Commission (2019) Excise duty tables—manufactured tobacco. https://ec.europa.eu/taxation_customs/sites/taxation/files/resources/documents/taxation/excise_duties/tobacco_products/rates/excise_duties-part_iii_tobacco_en.pdf. Accessed 24 Feb 2020

European Commission (2020a) Excise movement and control system. https://ec.europa.eu/taxation_customs/business/excise-duties-alcohol-tobacco-energy/excise-movement-control-system_en. Accessed 24 Feb 2020

European Commission (2020b) Overview—instrument for pre-accession assistance. European Commission, European Neighbourhood Policy and Enlargement Negotiations. https://ec.europa.eu/neighbourhood-enlargement/instruments/overview_en. Accessed 24 Feb 2020

Europol (2011) Large international operation against cigarette smuggling networks. Europol press release, 23 June 2011, The Hauge. https://www.europol.europa.eu/newsroom/news/large-international-operation-against-cigarette-smuggling-networks. Accessed 24 Feb 2020

Europol (2019) Operational task force leads to dismantling of one of Europe's most prolific crime groups behind €680 million operation. Europol Press Release, 22 May 2019. https://www.europol.europa.eu/newsroom/news/operational-task-force-leads-to-dismantling-of-one-of-europe%E2%80%99s-most-prolific-crime-groups-behind-%E2%82%AC680-million-operation. Accessed 24 Feb 2020

Europol (2020) Partners and agreements. https://www.europol.europa.eu/partners-agreements. Accessed 24 Feb 2020

Eurostat (2019) Comparative price levels for food, beverages and tobacco. Eurostat December 2019. http://ec.europa.eu/eurostat/statistics-explained/index.php/Comparative_price_levels_for_food,_beverages_and_tobacco#Food.2C_beverages_and_tobacco. Accessed 24 Feb 2020

Frontex (2018) 23 smugglers arrested, drugs and cigarettes seized during Frontex-led operation. Frontex News Release, 29 June 2018. https://frontex.europa.eu/media-centre/news-release/23-smugglers-arrested-drugs-and-cigarettes-seized-during-frontex-led-operation-PIk7rS. Accessed 24 Feb 2020

References

GATT (1994) General agreement on tariffs and trade 1994, Apr. 15, 1994, Marrakesh Agreement Establishing the World Trade Organization, Annex 1A, 1867 U.N.T.S. 187, 33 I.L.M. 1153

HM Customs and Excise and HM Treasury (2000) Tackling tobacco smuggling. The Stationery Office, London

HM Government (2019a) Guidance—check temporary rates of customs duty (tariffs) on imports after Brexit (subsequently withdrawn). https://www.gov.uk/guidance/check-temporary-rates-of-customs-duty-on-imports-after-eu-exit. Accessed 24 Feb 2020

HM Government (2019b) Guidance—the customs tariff (preferential trade agreement) (EU Exit) regulations 2019. https://www.gov.uk/government/publications/the-customs-tariff-preferential-trade-agreement-eu-exit-regulations-2019. Accessed 24 Feb 2020

HM Government (2020) Trade tariff database. https://www.trade-tariff.service.gov.uk/sections. Accessed 24 Feb 2020

HM Revenue and Customs (2009) Guidance—excise movement and control system: how to register and use. https://www.gov.uk/guidance/excise-movement-and-control-system-how-to-register-and-use. Accessed 24 Feb 2020

HM Revenue and Customs (2016) Excise notice 2003: tobacco duty—the raw tobacco approval scheme. Her Majesty's Revenue and Customs, 14 Dec 2016. https://www.gov.uk/government/publications/excise-notice-2003-tobacco-duty-the-raw-tobacco-approval-scheme/excise-notice-2003-tobacco-duty-the-raw-tobacco-approval-scheme. Accessed 24 Feb 2020

HM Revenue and Customs (2018a) Excise notice 2004: tobacco duty—tobacco products manufacturing machine licensing scheme. Her Majesty's Revenue and Customs, 25 Jan 2018. https://www.gov.uk/government/publications/excise-notice-2004-tobacco-duty-tobacco-products-manufacturing-machine-licensing-scheme/excise-notice-2004-tobacco-duty-tobacco-products-manufacturing-machine-licensing-scheme. Accessed 24 Feb 2020

HM Revenue and Customs (2018b) Tobacco duty: illicit trade protocol—licensing of tobacco manufacturing machinery. Her Majesty's Revenue and Customs, Policy Paper, updated 25 Jan 2018. https://www.gov.uk/government/publications/tobacco-duty-illicit-trade-protocol-licensing-of-tobacco-manufacturing-machinery/tobacco-duty-illicit-trade-protocol-licensing-of-tobacco-manufacturing-machinery. Accessed 24 Feb 2020

HM Revenue and Customs (2019a) UK tobacco duty statistics. https://assets.publishing.service.gov.uk/government/uploads/system/uploads/attachment_data/file/802697/2019_APR_Tobacco_Publication.pdf. Accessed 24 Feb 2020

HM Revenue and Customs (2019b) 2018–19 Annual report and accounts. Her Majesty's Revenue and Customs, 18 July 2019. https://assets.publishing.service.gov.uk/government/uploads/system/uploads/attachment_data/file/824652/HMRC_Annual_Report_and_Accounts_2018-19__web_.pdf. Accessed 24 Feb 2020

HM Revenue and Customs (2019c) Guidance: tobacco products duty rates—minimum excise duty for cigarettes (updated 29 Oct 2018). https://www.gov.uk/government/publications/rates-and-allowances-excise-duty-tobacco-duty/excise-duty-tobacco-duty-rates#minimum-excise-duty-for-cigarettes. Accessed 24 Feb 2020

HM Revenue and Customs (2019d) UK government guidance—Importing excise goods to the UK from the EU from 1 Jan 2021. https://www.gov.uk/guidance/importing-excise-goods-from-the-eu-in-a-no-deal-brexit Accessed 27 Feb 2020

HMRC and UK Border Force (2015) Tackling illicit tobacco: from leaf to light the HMRC and border force strategy to tackle tobacco smuggling. Government of the United Kingdom. https://assets.publishing.service.gov.uk/government/uploads/system/uploads/attachment_data/file/418732/Tackling_illicit_tobacco_-_From_leaf_to_light__2015_.pdf. Accessed 24 Feb 2020

Ilett N (2018) The illicit tobacco trade—what do we know? Stakeholder conference to fight illicit tobacco, 23 Mar 2018, Brussels, European Economic and Social Council. https://www.eesc.europa.eu/sites/default/files/files/nicholas_ilett_-_the_illicit_tobacco_trade_-_what_do_we_know.pdf. Accessed 24 Feb 2020

NHS (2018) Statistics on smoking—England, 2018. National Health Service Digital. https://digital.nhs.uk/data-and-information/publications/statistical/statistics-on-smoking/statistics-on-smoking-england-2018. Accessed 24 Feb 2020

Office for Budget Responsibility (2019) OBT tobacco duties. https://obr.uk/forecasts-in-depth/tax-by-tax-spend-by-spend/tobacco-duties/. Accessed 24 Feb 2020

Office of National Statistics (2020) RPI: Ave price—Cigarettes 20 king size filter. https://www.ons.gov.uk/economy/inflationandpriceindices/timeseries/czmp. Accessed 24 Feb 2020

OLAF (2018) The OLAF report 2017. European Anti-Fraud Office. https://ec.europa.eu/anti-fraud/sites/antifraud/files/olaf_report_2017_en.pdf. Accessed 24 Feb 2020

Policy Department for Citizens' Rights and Constitutional Affairs (2018) The EU-UK relationship beyond Brexit: options for Police Cooperation and Judicial Cooperation in Criminal Matters. European Parliament, Policy Department for Citizens' Rights and Constitutional Affairs, Directorate General for Internal Policies of the Union, Study, PE 604.975—July 2018. https://www.europarl.europa.eu/RegData/etudes/STUD/2018/604975/IPOL_STU(2018)604975_EN.pdf. Accessed 24 Feb 2020

Public Health England (2016) Tobacco products and e-cigarette cross-border sales registration. Public Health England Guidance, Published 28 Apr 2016, Last updated 4 Feb 2020. https://www.gov.uk/government/publications/tobacco-products-and-e-cigarette-cross-border-sales-registration. Accessed 24 Feb 2020

Public Health England (2020a) List of registered retailers. Public Health England Guidance, Updated 4 Feb 2020. https://www.gov.uk/government/publications/tobacco-products-and-e-cigarette-cross-border-sales-registration/list-of-registered-retailers. Accessed 24 Feb 2020

Public Health England (2020b) Member states that permit cross-border distance sales of tobacco and e-cigarette products. Public Health England Guidance, Updated 4 Feb 2020. https://www.gov.uk/government/publications/tobacco-products-and-e-cigarette-cross-border-sales-registration/member-states-that-permit-cross-border-distance-sales-of-e-cigarettes-andor-tobacco-products. Accessed 24 Feb 2020

Regulation (EU) 2016/1624 of the European Parliament and of the Council of 14 September 2016 on the European Border and Coast Guard and amending Regulation (EU) 2016/399 of the European Parliament and of the Council and repealing Regulation (EC) No 863/2007 of the European Parliament and of the Council, Council Regulation (EC) No 2007/2004 and Council Decision 2005/267/EC

Regulation (EU) 2018/1727 of the European Parliament and of the Council of 14 November 2018 on the European Union Agency for Criminal Justice Cooperation (Eurojust), and replacing and repealing Council Decision 2002/187/JHA. OJ L 295, 21.11.2018, pp 138–183

Regulation (EU) No 250/2014 of the European Parliament and of the Council of 26 February 2014 establishing a programme to promote activities in the field of the protection of the financial interests of the European Union (Hercule III programme) and repealing Decision No 804/2004/EC. OJ L 84, 20.3.2014, pp 6–13

Stuttaford D, Brain S (2018) VAT for businesses if there's no Brexit deal. Orton Rose Fullbright, Inside Brexit Blog, 24 Sept 2018. https://www.insidebrexitlaw.com/blog/vat-for-businesses-if-there-s-no-brexit-deal. Accessed 24 Feb 2020

The Raw Tobacco (Approval Scheme) Regulations 2016. UK Parliament. https://www.legislation.gov.uk/uksi/2016/1172/made. Accessed 24 Feb 2020

The Standardised Packaging of Tobacco Products Regulations 2015. UK Parliament. https://www.legislation.gov.uk/uksi/2015/829/contents/made. Accessed 24 Feb 2020

The temporary rates of customs duty (tariffs) on imports would not apply to goods crossing from Ireland into Northern Ireland. WTO The United Kingdom will make a further notification concerning the date of application of this draft Schedule XIX-United Kingdom. Until that date, the United Kingdom continues to be covered by the Schedule CLXXV-European Union (EU-28)

The Tobacco and Related Products Regulations 2016. UK Parliament. http://www.legislation.gov.uk/uksi/2016/507/contents/made. Accessed 24 Feb 2020

References

The Tobacco Products Manufacturing Machinery (Licensing Scheme) Regulations 2018. UK Parliament. https://www.legislation.gov.uk/uksi/2018/75/made. Accessed 24 Feb 2020

The Travellers' Allowances (Amendment) Order 2008. UK Parliament. https://www.legislation.gov.uk/uksi/2008/3058/contents/made. Accessed 24 Feb 2020

TMA (2017) TMA response to HMG's white paper on Customs. Tobacco Manufacturers' Association, 6 Nov 2017. http://the-tma.org.uk/wp-content/uploads/2017/11/TMA-response-to-HMG-customs-white-paper-Final.pdf. Accessed 24 Feb 2020

Tobacco Products (Descriptions of Products) Order 2003. UK Parliament. https://www.legislation.gov.uk/uksi/2003/1471/made. Accessed 24 Feb 2020

Tobacco Products Duty Act 1979 (as amended by Finance Act 2016). UK Parliament. https://www.legislation.gov.uk/ukpga/1979/7. Accessed 24 Feb 2020

UK Department of Health (1998) Smoking kills. A white paper on tobacco. Government of the United Kingdom, Department of Health. https://www.gov.uk/government/uploads/system/uploads/attachment_data/file/260754/4177.pdf. Accessed 24 Feb 2020

UK Department of Health (2017) Towards a smoke-free generation a tobacco control plan for England. Government of the United Kingdom, Department of Health, July 2017. https://www.gov.uk/government/publications/towards-a-smoke-free-generation-tobacco-control-plan-for-england. Accessed 24 Feb 2020

UK Parliament (2019) Background and Committee's conclusions on Proposal for a Regulation amending Regulation 883/2013 concerning investigations conducted by the European Anti-Fraud Office (OLAF) as regards cooperation with the European Public Prosecutor's Office and the effectiveness of OLAF investigations.UK Parliament, Commons Select Committees, European Scrutiny Committee, Document number (39775), 9313/18 + ADD 1, COM(18) 338. https://publications.parliament.uk/pa/cm201719/cmselect/cmeuleg/301-lxv/30112.htm. Accessed 24 Feb 2020

UK-IPO (2018) IP Crime and Enforcement Report 2017–2018. United Kingdom Intellectual Property Office. https://assets.publishing.service.gov.uk/government/uploads/system/uploads/attachment_data/file/740124/DPS-007593_IP_Crime_Report_2018_-_Web_v2.pdf. Accessed 24 Feb 2020

Value Added Tax Act 1994. UK Parliament. https://www.legislation.gov.uk/ukpga/1994/23/contents. Accessed 24 Feb 2020

Webb D (2019) UK progress in rolling over EU trade agreements. House of Commons Library, Briefing Paper Number 7792, 22 Aug 2019

World Bank (2019) Confronting illicit tobacco trade—a global review of country experiences, United Kingdom. World Bank. http://pubdocs.worldbank.org/en/248361548435105081/WBG-Tobacco-IllicitTrade-UnitedKingdom.pdf. Accessed 24 Feb 2020

Open Access This chapter is licensed under the terms of the Creative Commons Attribution 4.0 International License (http://creativecommons.org/licenses/by/4.0/), which permits use, sharing, adaptation, distribution and reproduction in any medium or format, as long as you give appropriate credit to the original author(s) and the source, provide a link to the Creative Commons license and indicate if changes were made.

The images or other third party material in this chapter are included in the chapter's Creative Commons license, unless indicated otherwise in a credit line to the material. If material is not included in the chapter's Creative Commons license and your intended use is not permitted by statutory regulation or exceeds the permitted use, you will need to obtain permission directly from the copyright holder.

Chapter 5
EU and Member States Agreements with the Tobacco Industry

Preventive policies against illicit trade include cooperation frameworks established by the EU and the Member States with tobacco manufacturers. Over the years, collaboration with tobacco companies has taken place under two main formats: (i) voluntary, non-binding memoranda of understanding (MoU) signed by Member States individually and tobacco manufacturers, and (ii) legally binding enforceable agreements concluded between the EU (and its Member States) and the four largest tobacco manufacturers. The fate of these agreements will impact the control of tobacco illicit trade in both the UK and EU more widely. This will depend of their questionable renewal generally and application by the UK post Brexit.

5.1 Voluntary Memoranda of Understanding

International tobacco companies and some EU countries entered into voluntary partnerships in the form of memoranda of understanding (MoUs). The declared objective of MoUs is to combat illicit tobacco trade. The MoU between Philip Morris International (PMI) and Italy concluded in 1999 was among the first such instrument which served as a basis for dozens of similar agreements. The exact number of MoUs signed between international tobacco companies and government agencies is unknown, and generally the text of such agreements are not publicly available. Recent estimates put the figure at around 120 (20 signed by British American Tobacco (BAT), 24 by Imperial, 30 by Japan Tobacco International (JTI), and 50 by PMI).[1]

---

[1] Crosbie et al. (2019) Memoranda of understanding: a tobacco industry strategy to undermine illicit tobacco trade policies.

In the specific case of the UK, the first MoU was signed in 2002 by Gallaher (later purchased by JTI) with HMC&E (today HMCR).[2] The general focus of the MoU, which is publicly accessible, is on cooperation and data sharing with the objective of limiting trade in smuggled and counterfeit goods. Although not binding, the MoU contains specific obligations. For instance, Gallaher undertakes to only supply products where there is a legitimate demand for the product in the intended final markets and where information indicates any substantial smuggling of its products, to take action to identify the supply routes and suspected export trade. Under the MoU, the company also has to refuse sales where the end-sale (consumption) destination is in doubt, revisit and where necessary discontinue the relationship with any particular distributor if it discovers improper behaviour. It has to immediately terminate the trading relationship if it concludes that any distributor is a smuggler of Gallaher products or that the distributor is knowingly or recklessly supplying a smuggler with such products. Also, pursuant to the MoU, Gallaher provides Customs, upon request, with all relevant information about the intended destination of export consignments as well as prompt access to export sales data.

Between 2002 and 2003, the UK Government signed similar MoUs with BAT, JTI and in Imperial Tobacco (now Imperial Brands plc). Like the MoU with Gallaher, the other MoUs focus on cooperation and information sharing, with a view of minimising the presence of the company's brands in the UK illicit market. None of these instruments creates binding legal obligations or foresees enforcement mechanisms.

The MoUs have attracted criticism.[3] Some commentators have expressed concerns with regard to the non-transparent character of such instruments—thus potentially contravening FCTC Article 5.3 and the ITP. More generally, some have argued that international tobacco companies have promoted the conclusion of MoUs as a way to create connections with governments mainly to pre-empt more stringent regulation of illicit trade. Also, some have remarked that since MoUs are, by definition, not binding, they do not create accountability system or penalties for non-compliance, rendering them ineffective at controlling illicit trade.[4]

The MoUs signed by the UK and currently in force should remain unaffected by Brexit, irrespective of the modalities of the UK's withdrawal from the EU. The MoUs have been concluded by the UK Government/HMRC and neither the EU nor any EU institution or agency is a party to them. Also, contrary to the binding agreements discussed below, since the MoUs are not legally binding, the UK can unilaterally withdraw from them at any time.

---

[2]The text of the MoU is contained in a memorandum submitted by Gallaher Group Plc as written evidence ordered by the House of Commons in 2005. See UK Parliament (2005) Memorandum submitted by Gallaher Group Plc.
[3]Crosbie et al. (2019).
[4]Ibid.

5.2 Binding Agreements

The MoUs described above should not be confounded with the legally binding and enforceable agreements concluded between the EU and the Member States, including the UK, on the one hand, and the world's four largest tobacco manufacturers on the other hand. In total, the EU and the Member States have signed four such agreements, three of which are still in force. The first one was signed in 2004 with PMI—the 'Anti-Contraband and Anti-Counterfeit Agreement and General Release'. It expired in 2016 without being renewed. The agreements with JTI are supposed to remain in place until 2022, whereas those with BAT and Imperial Tobacco are due to end in 2030. The texts of the agreements are available on the OLAF website.[5]

Under the terms of the four agreements, tobacco manufacturers agreed to pay a collective total of \$2.15 billion to the EU and to the Member States countries participating in the agreements with the objective of fighting cigarette smuggling and counterfeiting. The agreements also create obligations for tobacco manufacturers to prevent their products from falling into the hands of criminals, notably by supplying only those quantities required by the legitimate market, taking care that they sell to legitimate clients only ('know your customer' programs). They also have to implement a tracking system to help law enforcement authorities if cigarettes are traded illegally. Further, the agreements provide that companies shall compensate the European Commission and the Member States for lost taxes, duties, and other costs if the authorities seize illicit tobacco products that are not counterfeit and provide funding for anti-smuggling and anti-counterfeiting initiatives.

For instance, in the 2006–2015 period PMI paid a total of €2,275,471.07 for seizures in relation to the UK. Of this total figure, €2,173,456.89 went to the UK, whereas the remaining balance of €102,014.18 went to the EU. During the same period, the grand total (EU-wide) paid by PMI for seizures under the agreement amounted to €68,228,115.38.[6]

The agreements have drawn criticism from some authors since inception.[7] Indeed, some agreements were negotiated to settle or avoid legal disputes between tobacco manufacturers and the EU in relation to the involvement of the former in smuggling and money laundering. Regarding their usefulness in the fight against the evolving illicit trade in tobacco products, in 2016, the EU Commission published an assessment of the agreement with PMI.[8] Although specific to the agreement with PMI, by and large the same findings apply to the other agreements as well. The EU Commission's assessment found that the PMI Agreement made an important contribution to fighting PMI illicit trade in the past. At the same time, it acknowledged how the

---

[5] See OLAF (2018) Tobacco Smuggling. Sweden did not sign the BAT and ITL agreements.

[6] Member States received 90.3% of payments whereas 9.7% went to the general EU budget. See European Commission (2016) Technical assessment of PMI Agreement and General Release, Annex 1—PMI Seizures Payments EU and Member State Shares.

[7] Joossens et al. (2016) Assessment of the European Union's illicit trade agreements with the four major Transnational Tobacco Companies.

[8] See European Commission (2016) Technical assessment of PMI Agreement and General Release.

market and legislative framework have changed significantly since the entry into force of the Agreement.

The illicit market has undergone significant changes. Therefore, in its assessment, the EU Commission questioned the very relevance of such an instrument in light of the surge of cheap (illicit) '*whites*', taking into account the administrative and reputational costs to public authorities resulting from the cooperation with tobacco manufacturers.[9] The tobacco control and anti-illicit trade legislative setting has also evolved considerably since the entry into force of the PMI Agreement in 2004. The EU Commission's assessment highlights the limits of the PMI Agreement—and consequently of the other agreements as well—in effectively tackling today's illicit trade. In particular, TPD-2 introduces new tools in the fight against the illicit trade of tobacco products, as described in Sect. 6.1 below. The EU Commission's assessment nevertheless acknowledges that the PMI Agreement offers a global geographic scope concerning tracking at a master case level, but has only achieved partial global coverage in terms of marking at the pack level.[10] Finally, the assessment finds that other important aspects regulated in the PMI Agreement, such as due diligence, anti-money laundering, seizure payments, and supports investigators, will be largely covered by new future rules under the FCTC Protocol.

To date, three agreements signed by the EU *and* the Member States, including the UK, remain in force. The *JTI Agreement*,[11] together with the *Mutual Cessation Agreement* and the *Agreement regarding Gallaher*, was made on 14 December 2007 and binds JT International SA, JT International Holding BV, the EC, and the EU Member States.[12] For the EC, the MoU was signed by the Commission (double signature Director General of the legal service and the Director General of OLAF). The JTI Agreement will expire on 14 December 2022. The *BAT Agreement*,[13] made on 15 July 2010, binds British-American Tobacco (Holdings) Ltd, the EU, and 24 Member States. It will remain in force until 15 July 2030. *The ITL Agreement*,[14] made on 27 September 2010, binds Imperial Tobacco Ltd, the EU, and certain Member States. It should remain in force until 27 September 2030. In light of the outcome of the assessment of the agreement with PMI, it appears likely that the Commission will take the same view in respect of the other three Agreements currently in force.

---

[9] Ibid p. 29.

[10] Ibid p. 30.

[11] The agreement is available online at OLAF (2016) Japan Tobacco 2007.

[12] The agreements were all executed on 14 December 2007. 26 Member States signed the agreements on the execution date; the UK signed the agreements in April 2009. The EU took over the legal obligations of the EC in December 2009.

[13] The agreement is available at OLAF (2016) British American Tobacco (BAT) 2010.

[14] The agreement is available at OLAF (2016) Imperial Tobacco Limited (ITL) 2010.

5.2 Binding Agreements

The three EU binding agreements with the manufacturers will stop applying with regard to the UK after Brexit day. Should the UK nevertheless consider maintaining such instruments, parties could negotiate a 'roll over'. The UK could thus become a stand-alone party in subsequent agreements with large tobacco manufacturers that mirror the content of the original ones. The UK has already negotiated the 'roll over' of several free trade agreements it has subscribed to as an EU Member, as discussed in Section 4 above. However, if the UK will consider the conclusions reached by the EU Commission on this topic, the request for post-Brexit industry agreements may have to come from the industry itself proving their continued relevance. As pointed out in the Commission's assessment, ITP has a global reach and *"contains many provisions broadly similar to those of the tobacco agreements"*.[15] Beside the questions relating to the actual need for such formal cooperation, any involvement of the industry risks facing considerable challenges by various stakeholder groups, including under Art. 5.3 of the FCTC requiring protection of tobacco control policies from commercial and other vested interests of the tobacco industry.[16]

References

Crosbie E, Bialous S, and Glantz SA (2019) Memoranda of understanding: a tobacco industry strategy to undermine illicit tobacco trade policies. In: BMJ Journals, Tobacco Control, Published Online First: 18 Jan 2019. https://tobaccocontrol.bmj.com/content/tobaccocontrol/early/2019/01/18/tobaccocontrol-2018-054668.full.pdf?ijkey=rF5sMQ7tKIfiniE&keytype=ref. Accessed 24 Feb 2020

European Commission (2016) Technical assessment of the experience made with the anti-contraband and anti-counterfeit agreement and general release of 9 July 2004 among Philip Morris International and affiliates, the Union and its Member States. European Commission Staff Working Paper, Brussels, 24 Feb 2016, SWD (2016) 44 final. https://ec.europa.eu/anti-fraud/sites/antifraud/files/technical_assessment_pmi_24022016_en.pdf. Accessed 24 Feb 2020

Joossens L, Gilmore AB, Stoklosa M, and Ross H (2016) Assessment of the European Union's illicit trade agreements with the four major transnational Tobacco companies. In: BMJ Journals Tobacco Control vol 25(3), pp 255–260. https://tobaccocontrol.bmj.com/content/25/3/254. Accessed 24 Feb 2020

OLAF (2016) British American Tobacco (BAT) 2010. European Anti-Fraud Office. https://ec.europa.eu/anti-fraud/investigations/eu-revenue/bat_en. Accessed 24 Feb 2020

OLAF (2016) Imperial Tobacco Limited (ITL) 2010. European Anti-Fraud Office. https://ec.europa.eu/anti-fraud/investigations/eu-revenue/imperial_tobacco_en. Accessed 24 Feb 2020

OLAF (2016) Japan tobacco 2007. European Anti-Fraud Office. https://ec.europa.eu/anti-fraud/investigations/eu-revenue/japan_tobacco_2007_en. Accessed 24 Feb 2020

OLAF (2018) Tobacco smuggling. European Anti-Fraud Office. https://ec.europa.eu/anti-fraud/investigations/eu-revenue/cigarette_smuggling_en. Accessed 24 Feb 2020

---

[15] European Commission (2016) Technical assessment of PMI Agreement and General Release, p. 7.

[16] Art. 5.3 of the FCTC reads *"In setting and implementing their public health policies with respect to tobacco control, Parties shall act to protect these policies from commercial and other vested interests of the tobacco industry in accordance with national law."*.

UK Parliament (2005) Memorandum submitted by Gallaher Group Plc. Select committee on treasury written evidence. https://publications.parliament.uk/pa/cm200405/cmselect/cmtreasy/126/126we20.htm. Accessed 24 Feb 2020

Open Access This chapter is licensed under the terms of the Creative Commons Attribution 4.0 International License (http://creativecommons.org/licenses/by/4.0/), which permits use, sharing, adaptation, distribution and reproduction in any medium or format, as long as you give appropriate credit to the original author(s) and the source, provide a link to the Creative Commons license and indicate if changes were made.

The images or other third party material in this chapter are included in the chapter's Creative Commons license, unless indicated otherwise in a credit line to the material. If material is not included in the chapter's Creative Commons license and your intended use is not permitted by statutory regulation or exceeds the permitted use, you will need to obtain permission directly from the copyright holder.

Chapter 6
Key EU and Global Anti-illicit Trade Initiatives

Two initiatives in particular, one at EU level and one with global reach promoted by the World Health Organization, currently steer the efforts against illicit trade in tobacco products in the UK. Both are likely to continue to apply after Brexit implementation in the UK. The two instruments are the *2014 EU Tobacco Products Directive* ('TPD-2') and the *WHO FCTC Protocol to Eliminate Illicit Trade in Tobacco Products* ('ITP'). Despite differences in their respective subject matter and geographical scope, the two instruments share several commonalities. Most notably, a key element of the ITP—the establishment of a tracking and tracing system (Art. 8)—is a cornerstone of the 2014 TPD-2, and of the EU-wide effort to tackle illicit tobacco trade.

6.1 2014 EU Tobacco Products Directive (TPD-2)

The 2014 Tobacco Products Directive (TPD-2)[1] repeals and replaces the previous legal framework, set out in *Directive 2001/37/EC*.[2] TPD-2 brings substantial changes to reflect scientific, market, and international developments, and its adoption marked a pivotal development in tobacco control policy in the EU.

The scope of TPD-2 is broad. The Directive aims at improving the functioning of the internal market for tobacco products by approximating laws, regulations, and administrative provisions of the EU Member States in a wide range of areas. Approximation is, for instance, required with regard to the ingredients and emissions of tobacco products and related reporting obligations, including the maximum emission levels for tar, nicotine, and carbon monoxide for cigarettes; certain aspects

---

[1] Directive 2014/40/EU on the approximation of the laws, regulations and administrative provisions of the Member States concerning the manufacture, presentation and sale of tobacco and related products (and repealing Directive 2001/37/EC).

[2] Directive 2001/37/EC on the approximation of the laws, regulations and administrative provisions of the Member States concerning the manufacture, presentation and sale of tobacco products.

© The Author(s) 2020
M. Foltea, *Brexit and the Control of Tobacco Illicit Trade*,
SpringerBriefs in Law, https://doi.org/10.1007/978-3-030-45979-6_6

of the labelling and packaging of tobacco products including the health warnings that are to appear on unit packets of tobacco products, and any outside packaging as well as traceability and security features that are applied to tobacco products to ensure their compliance with TPD-2; cross-border distance sales of tobacco products; and the obligation to submit a notification for novel tobacco products.[3]

The issue of illicit tobacco trade figures prominently among the objectives of TPD-2, and select elements of TPD-2 are essential components of the EU Commission's 2nd action plan to implement the 2013 strategy *'Stepping up the fight against cigarette smuggling and other forms of illicit trade in tobacco products—a comprehensive EU strategy'*.[4]

The Preamble to TPD-2 acknowledges how "considerable volumes of illicit products, which do not fulfil the requirements laid down in [the precedent framework under] Directive 2001/37/EC, are placed on the market and there are indications that these volumes might increase. Such illicit products undermine the free circulation of compliant products and the protection provided for by tobacco control legislation."[5] The Preamble also makes explicit reference to the WHO Framework Convention on Tobacco Control (FCTC) and to how the provisions of the FCTC—including those that deal with illicit trade—are binding on the Union and its Member States, and how legislative action is required to implement the FCTC.[6]

A key goal of TPD-2, as specified in its Preamble, is the introduction of security features that will facilitate the verification of whether or not tobacco products are authentic, as well as the need to track and trace the movements of tobacco products throughout the EU.[7] The implementation of two key provision of TPD-2, i.e. Articles 15 ('Traceability') and 16 ('Security Features'), aims at reducing the availability of illicit supplies by increasing the security of the legal supply chain. The EU traceability system is the first regional system of its kind and applies to tobacco products manufactured in the EU as well as those manufactured outside of the EU which are placed on the EU market. The system allows for the monitoring of the current location of a product within the supply chain, creation of a time and location record for all movement of that product (tracking), as well as identifying the past locations of a product in order to verify the product route back to its origin (tracing).[8]

The system does not track and trace the movement of illicit tobacco. Rather, the accurate tracking of legal tobacco products would allow authorities to determine when a product has diverted into the illicit market. The traceability system contributes

---

[3] Article 1, Directive 2014/40/EU.

[4] European Commission (2018) Communication on 2nd Action Plan to fight the illicit tobacco trade 2018–2022.

[5] Preamble recital. 29, Directive 2014/40/EU.

[6] Preamble recital 7, Directive 2014/40/EU.

[7] Preamble recital 29, Directive 2014/40/EU. A system developed to standardize quality management systems, traceability of products can be construed as the ability to track a product forward through specified stages of the supply chain down to the consumers and simultaneously to retrace the history and locations of the product back to its original production line.

[8] For a detailed description of the system see European Commission (2017) Impact Assessment on Implementing Regulation on traceability system and security features for tobacco products.

6.1 2014 EU Tobacco Products Directive (TPD-2)

to reducing the circulation of non-compliant tobacco products (i.e. products that do not meet all legal requirements in terms of content, packaging, and duty payable), and thus reducing artificially cheap supplies of illegal tobacco products, and hence protecting public health, state budgets and legitimate economic activities.

In a nutshell, the traceability system under TPD-2 Article 15 foresees that all individual packets of tobacco products—either manufactured in the EU or manufactured outside the EU and placed on the EU market—shall be marked with a unique identifier. Relevant economic operators (such as manufacturers, importers and wholesalers), involved in tobacco trade record the movements of these packets throughout the supply chain and transmit the related information to an independent third-party data storage facility who will record and store this data.[9] The collected data is made accessible to authorities of the EU countries and to the EU Commission for enforcement purposes.

Under the EU traceability system, the generation of unique identifiers, as well as of all other codes required for pre-registration of economic operators, facilities and machines, is entrusted to designated 'ID issuers' who are required to be financially and legally independent from the tobacco industry.[10] The appointed 'ID issuers' receive requests to generate unique identifiers from manufacturers and importers of tobacco products. Unique identifiers are applied to the unit packet after being encoded in an authorized data carrier. Correctly marked unit packets can then be tracked and traced throughout the supply chain. Tracking and tracing at an aggregated level (cartons, master cases, or pallets) is also permitted, provided the unit packets remain traceable. Transportation between different facilitate is also regulated. Each dispatch and arrival must be recorded and reported to the repositories system, up to the point of dispatch to the first retail outlet, i.e. the first place where products will be made available to consumers. Another requirement of TPD-2, set out in Article 16, foresees that all individual packets of tobacco products placed on the EU market shall carry a tamper-proof security feature to protect the process of verifying unique identifiers following their applications, composed of visible and invisible elements.[11]

The impact assessment prepared by the Commission in 2017 provides some examples of how the systems under TPD-2 Articles 15 and 16 may contribute in practice to addressing illicit tobacco trade.[12] For instance, consider if a dispatch truck fails to arrive at its next expected destination along the supply chain. By accessing the

---

[9] Article 15(5) of the TPD requires that all economic operators, from the manufacturer to the last economic operator before the first retail outlet, record the entry of all unit packets into their possession, as well as all intermediate movements and the final exit of the unit packets from their possession.

[10] ID issuers are sometimes referred to as the 'guardian of uniqueness'.

[11] Commission Implementing Regulation (EU) 2018/574 requires that the verification of unit level unique identifiers is protected with an anti-tampering device supplied and installed by an independent third party. The independence of the third party must be attested by submitting to the relevant Member States and to the Commission a declaration attesting the compliance of that third party with the requirements on independence, as set out in the Regulation.

[12] European Commission (2017) Impact Assessment on Implementing Regulation on traceability system and security features for tobacco products, p. 6.

stored traceability information, authorities will be in a position to determine where the last recorded movements of the products in question took place. This will help to pinpoint the exact point of diversion (contraband). Similarly, regular dispatches to a specific retail outlet are suddenly cancelled or significantly reduced at the request of the retailer, due to reduced demand. By accessing the stored traceability information, authorities will be able to monitor such unexpected fluctuations and investigate whether they are due to increased circulation of illicit products in the area concerned (for example sale of counterfeit or illicit *white* products in a certain area or by a certain retailer).

Another example is when tobacco products which do not carry security features, or whose security features have been tampered with or compromised, or are otherwise noncompliant, are identified by consumers or owners of retail outlets in which they are placed on the market. The consumers or retailer outlet have been alerted to the fact that these products are likely to have emanated from illicit trade and are in a position to take appropriate action and inform authorities.

TPD-2 required the system of traceability as well as the security features to be in place by 20 May 2019 for cigarettes and hand rolling tobacco (HRT), and by 20 May 2024 for all other tobacco products. The technical aspects are set out in the EU *Commission Implementing Regulation (EU 2018/574)* which provides the details for both systems.[13]

On 21 December 2018, the EU Commission selected, among the list of approved repository providers, Dentsu Aegis Network AG (DAN AG) as the provider of the 'secondary repository'. Each Member State was required to appoint a national ID issuer, the entity responsible for issuing unique identifiers, and registering economic operators, facilities, and machines in the system. On 27 February 2019, De La Rue announced that it has been retained by the UK Government to be the UK's ID Issuer.[14] The five-year contract will see De La Rue implement a digital solution to track and trace the approximately 1.7 billion cigarette and hand rolling tobacco packs sold in the UK each year through a unique identifier.

The *Tobacco Products (Traceability and Security Features) Regulations 2019*,[15] which came into force on 20 May 2019, is the secondary legislation that

---

[13] Commission Implementing Regulation (EU) 2018/574 on technical standards for the establishment and operation of a traceability system for tobacco products. The EU Commission has prepared additional implementing acts regarding both the traceability system and the security features, namely the Commission Delegated Regulation (EU) 2018/573 of 15 December 2017 on key elements of data storage contracts to be concluded as part of a traceability system for tobacco products; and Commission Implementing Decision (EU) 2018/576 of 15 December 2017 on technical standards for security features applied to tobacco products.

[14] See TED (2019) United Kingdom-Salford: Software package and information systems, Contract award notice, and De La Rue (2019).

[15] Commission Implementing Decision (EU) 2018/576 of 15 December 2017 on technical standards for security features applied to tobacco products.

6.1 2014 EU Tobacco Products Directive (TPD-2)

implements the TPD in the UK. In particular, it implements TPD-2 Article 15 (Traceability) and Article 16 (Security feature), as well as TPD-2 Article 23 (Cooperation and enforcement). The Regulations also implement the *Commission Implementing Decision (EU) 2018/576 of 15 December 2017 on technical standards for security features applied to tobacco products*.

The UK is a final destination for illicit tobacco products and the information available suggest that a significant share of such products transit via (if they do not originate from) EU Member States. 'Track and trace' establishes a system that provides public authorities and law enforcement with a key tool to keep track of products entering the EU and circulating within it.

The *Tobacco Products (Traceability and Security Features) Regulations* 2019 translates into UK law, the track and trace system, as well as the security feature requirements mandated by the TPD. While both systems can function outside of the EU at the country level, the track and trace system delegates certain tasks to the EU Commission and requires that notifications related to the system be sent to Brussels as well.

There is some confusion over the potential implication of Brexit on the track and trace system. In September 2019 the media reported the possibility of a one year suspension of the track and trace system in the UK in case of a '*Hard Brexit*' on 31 October 2019.[16] The same sources reported that during such period, the UK would try to introduce a UK 'stand-alone' system which would give full regulatory control to the UK. While as a non-EU member (unless taking part in the single market) the UK can remodel the track and trace system without taking into account the requirements set out in the relevant EU legislation, any modification will have to guarantee that the system remains interoperable with the other ITP signatories, as described in Sect. 6.2 below. Systems should be able to 'talk' to each other, in particular systems that may be implemented in the principal sources of illicit trade found in the UK, and the mechanism put in place within the EU may well set a precedent for the implementation of these aspects of the ITP by other countries. It is therefore likely that any amendment to the UK track and trace system will not significantly depart from the EU system currently in place.

Should the UK instead opt for a '*Soft Brexit*', it will remain bound by EU TPD-2, including the track and trace requirements. Considered necessary to facilitate the smooth functioning of the internal market for tobacco and related products, the implementation of the track and trace system is also required from non-EU members that participate in the single market.[17]

---

[16] See Walker (2019) citing an HMRC spokesperson. See also TJI (2019) Track and Trace system to be suspended in no-deal Brexit.

[17] The process of incorporating the 2014 EU Tobacco Products Directive into the EEA Agreement is currently ongoing.

6.2 WHO FCTC Protocol to Eliminate Illicit Trade in Tobacco Products (ITP)

One of the most prominent global initiatives to tackle illicit tobacco trade at the international level is promoted by the World Health Organization (WHO).[18] The *WHO Framework Convention on Tobacco Control* (FCTC) is an international treaty designed to reduce tobacco-related deaths and disease by fostering international health cooperation in the area of tobacco control.[19] The EU, as well as the UK, ratified the FCTC. In total, 181 parties have done so to date, covering over 90% of the world's population, 70% of tobacco leaf growers, 70% of cigarette production, 70% of cigarette consumption, and over 60% of cigarette exporters.[20]

FCTC Article 15 obliges the Parties to develop a Protocol to tackle the illicit trade in tobacco products. After four years of negotiations, the Intergovernmental Negotiating Body (INB) set up to negotiate the Protocol, reached a consensus on the text in November 2012. Legally linked to the FCTC, the *Protocol to Eliminate Illicit Trade in Tobacco Products* (ITP), is the first multilateral treaty to specifically tackle illicit tobacco trade.[21] ITP entered into force on 25 September 2018 and currently has 58 Parties.[22] The ITP was open for signatures from 10 January 2013 to 9 January 2014. The EU signed the Protocol on 20 December 2013 and ratified it on 24 June 2014. The UK signed the Protocol on 17 December 2013 but only ratified it on 28 June 2018.[23] ITP represents a significant step towards a new global standard in tobacco control, with international partners working together to tackle the issue. It introduces a framework for general information sharing,[24] enforcement information sharing,[25] mutual administrative assistance,[26] mutual legal assistance,[27] and tracking and tracing information.[28]

ITP's own governance is embodied in the Meeting of the Parties (MOP).[29] In its first session, the MOP established a working group on the tracking and tracing system following Article 8, and a second one on assistance and cooperation following

---

[18] WHO Framework Convention on Tobacco Control (FCTC). World Health Organization, adopted 21 May 2003 and entered into force on 27 February 2004.

[19] The WHO FCTC is a free-standing convention, separate from the WHO itself.

[20] The list of Parties to the FCTC can be found at https://www.who.int/fctc/signatories_parties/en/.

[21] Protocol to Eliminate Illicit Trade in Tobacco Products. Adopted by the Conference of the Parties to the WHO FCTC, 2012.

[22] The list of Parties to the Protocol can be found at https://treaties.un.org/pages/ViewDetails.aspx?src=TREATY&mtdsg_no=IX-4-a&chapter=9&lang=en.

[23] See HM Government (2018) UK ratifies global treaty to tackle illegal tobacco trade.

[24] See Protocol Article 20.

[25] See Protocol Article 21.

[26] See Protocol Article 28.

[27] See Protocol Article 29.

[28] See Protocol Article 8.

[29] The work of the MOP is regulated by its own Rules of Procedure, agreed during the MOP first session, which was held in Geneva on 8–10 October 2018.

Articles 12, 21, 23, 24, 28 and 29. Parties participate in the discussions in the MOP as well as in the different working groups. Discussions are attended by Parties' government officials from different sectors relevant for ITP implementation, including health, customs, justice, finance, and trade, as well as representatives of intergovernmental organizations, including the World Customs Organization, the World Bank, and the WHO, and also members of civil society. The UK attends the Meetings of the Parties (MOPs) as well as the expert and working groups with its own delegates.

In an Exploratory Memorandum published in the run up to the UK ratification, the Exchequer Secretary to the Treasury noted how "most of the requirements of the Protocol have been in place in the UK for some time as part of our successful tobacco anti-fraud strategy."[30] With regard to the impact of the ITP on UK legislation, in 2013 HMRC found that "the UK already has legislation dealing with many of the subject areas covered by the Protocol. However, not all of the provisions are legislated for and some changes may be necessary".[31] On the same occasion, HMRC also noted that the ITP will apply to Gibraltar.[32] The licensing of tobacco product manufacturing machinery was the final outstanding requirement for the UK, and was fulfilled with the adoption of the Tobacco Products Manufacturing Machinery (Licensing Scheme) Regulations in 2018.[33]

Another key ITP requirement—the establishment of a global tracking and tracing regime for tobacco products within five years from the entry into force of the Protocol, as set out in ITP Article 9—was being rolled out by the UK as part of the implementation of the *EU Tobacco Products Directive 2014* (see Sect. 6.1 above). Following the UK's ratification of the ITP, the UK Government underlined how global standards, when in place, can make it harder for organised criminal gangs to profit. It also stressed the annual costs of illicit tobacco in terms of tax gaps, as well as the link between illicit tobacco trade and wider tobacco control efforts.[34]

ITP is a multilateral agreement, i.e. an international treaty to which three or more sovereign states are parties. For the purpose of EU law, as discussed below, since ITP includes areas of competence of the EU as well as those retained by the Member States, ITP was established as a 'mixed agreement'.[35] Both the EU and the Member States are parties to the Protocol. The EU signed the ITP in late 2013, paving the way for ratification of the agreement by EU Member States. The UK signed and ratified ITP on 17 December 2013 and on 28 June 2018, respectively. At the moment of ratification of the Protocol, the EU submitted a 'Declaration of Competences',

---

[30] See HM Government (2018) Explanatory Memorandum on the Protocol to Eliminate Illicit Trade in Tobacco Products.

[31] HMRC, "Explanatory Memorandum on European Union Documents", 12605/13, COM (2013)538, July 2013, regarding the signing of the ITP, para. 13.

[32] HMRC, "Explanatory Memorandum on European Union Documents", 12605/13, COM (2013)538, July 2013, regarding the signing of the ITP, para. 14.

[33] See Sect. 4.1.3 above.

[34] See HM Government (2018) UK ratifies global treaty to tackle illegal tobacco trade.

[35] With respect to the conclusion of international agreements, for the policy areas listed in TFEU Article 3(1), only the EU has the competence to act, whereas for the policy areas listed in Article 4(2) TFEU the EU and its Member States share competence.

which specifies the extent to which the Member States of the EU have conferred competences upon the EU in the areas covered by the ITP and the areas in which the EU and the Member States may legislate and adopt legally binding acts.[36]

The UK is bound by the ITP given that it is a party in its own right. Having ratified the Protocol before 10 July 2018, it enjoys its full rights. This is becaue the UK will remain a party to mixed multilateral agreements after it withdraws from the EU, where it is already a party in its own right, regardless of how Brexit will be conducted.[37] In preparation for the signing of the ITP in 2013 by the EU, HMRC pointed out how:

> [t]he UK will be party to the Protocol in its own right and could legislate, as necessary, without EU legislation. However, the movement and control of excise goods is administered at EU level with Directives and Regulations setting out the procedures for the holding and movement of those goods. Since the key aim of the Protocol is to combat illicit cross-border trade in tobacco and tobacco products, it is logical to legislate at EU level to ensure consistent treatment of businesses and the movement of excise goods between Member States.[38]

Article 129 (Specific arrangements relating to the Union's external action) of the *2019 Withdrawal Agreement* specifies that "*[…] during the transition period, the United Kingdom shall be bound by the obligations stemming from the international agreements concluded by the Union, by Member States acting on its behalf, or by the Union and its Member States acting jointly […]*". Para. 2 of the same provision adds that "*[d]uring the transition period, representatives of the United Kingdom shall not participate in the work of any bodies set up by international agreements concluded by the Union, or by Member States acting on its behalf, or by the Union and its Member States acting jointly, unless: (a) the United Kingdom participates in its own right.*"

Underlying the importance of Gibraltar for illicit tobacco trade, the *2019 Withdrawal Agreement Protocol on Gibraltar* states in Art. 3 para. 3 that:

> The United Kingdom shall ensure that its ratification of the Framework Convention on Tobacco Control, adopted in Geneva on 21 May 2003, and the Protocol to Eliminate Illicit Trade in Tobacco Products, adopted in Seoul on 12 November 2012, is extended to Gibraltar by 30 June 2020.[39]

As a party to the ITP, the rights and obligations of the UK after Brexit will remain unchanged. As a target market for illicit product, the UK is interested in widespread adoption of supply chain controls, beyond the EU region, in particular to reduce the supply of legitimate products in the UK illicit market. The ITP's impact on the level of illicit trade globally is dependent upon third countries signing and implementing

---

[36] The 'Declaration of Competences' has been prepared pursuant to ITP Article 44 (Ratification, acceptance, approval, formal confirmation or accession).

[37] HMRC, "Explanatory Memorandum on European Union Documents", 12605/13, COM (2013)538, July 2013, regarding the signing of the ITP.

[38] HMRC, "Explanatory Memorandum on European Union Documents", 12605/13, COM (2013)538, July 2013, regarding the signing of the ITP, para. 17.

[39] On the specific arrangement with regard to Gibraltar see Sect. 2.4 above.

it fully and effectively. Securing the global tobacco supply chain will make it easier for enforcement agencies and authorities to potentially detect both the point where products are diverted to the illicit market, and the people and entities involved with such acts.

The interests of the UK and of the EU in the implementation of the Protocol seem to be well aligned, as requested under Article 129 para. 3 of the *2019 Withdrawal Agreement* which specifies that the UK "*[i]n accordance with the principle of sincere cooperation, [...] shall refrain, during the transition period, from any action or initiative which is likely to be prejudicial to the Union's interests, in particular in the framework of any international organisation, agency, conference or forum of which the United Kingdom is a party in its own right.*" The ITP appears in the anti-illicit tobacco trade strategies of both the EU and the UK. The EU Commission's 2nd Action Plan to fight illicit tobacco trade (2018–2022) proposes to fully exploit the potential of the new FCTC Protocol as a global instrument and forum to curb the illicit tobacco trade, by taking a leading role in its implementation. The same vision emerges from the HMRC and Border Force strategy to tackle tobacco smuggling '*Tackling illicit tobacco: From leaf to light*', which underlines how the UK has "*championed international initiatives, such as the WHO Framework Convention on Tobacco Control, designed to reduce tobacco related deaths and disease, and the related Illicit Trade Protocol aimed at making further inroads into the global trade in illicit tobacco*".[40]

For the time being, the effects of the recently introduced track and trace system required by TPD-2 on illicit trade in tobacco products could prove rather modest as most of this trade originates from outside of the EU. For the track and trace system to fully deploy its effects, it would have to apply on a global basis, in particular in the source and transit countries; this is the stated objective of the ITP. In particular, and as acknowledged by the EU Commission, the ITP's potential in reducing illicit tobacco trade in the EU in the form of *illicit whites* cannot be underestimated. Indeed, many products considered *illicit whites* in the EU are legal products in their respective countries of origin. If those countries were to implement the ITP, including the track and trace system it requires, the supply of *illicit whites* may be substantially reduced.[41]

Both initiatives discussed above have a supranational character. They acknowledge how illicit trade in tobacco products transcends borders, thus requiring a coordinated response. Post-Brexit UK could do away with track and trace system (unless of course it chooses to remain in the single market). In practice, however, this is unlikely to happen. Indeed, the UK remains bound by ITP's obligations including Art. 8 which requires that the parties put in place a "*a global tracking and tracing regime, comprising national and/or regional tracking and tracing systems*".

---

[40] HMRC and UK Border Force (2015) Tackling illicit tobacco: From leaf to light The HMRC and Border Force strategy to tackle tobacco smuggling.

[41] European Commission (2018) Communication on 2nd Action Plan to fight the illicit tobacco trade 2018–2022.

References

Commission Delegated Regulation (EU) 2018/573 of 15 December 2017 on key elements of data storage contracts to be concluded as part of a traceability system for tobacco products; and Commission Implementing Decision (EU) 2018/576 of 15 December 2017 on technical standards for security features applied to tobacco products. OJ l96/1, pp 1–6, 16 Mar 2018

Commission Implementing Regulation (EU) 2018/574 of 15 December 2017 on technical standards for the establishment and operation of a traceability system for tobacco products, C/2017/8429, OJ L 96, pp 7–55, 16 Mar 2018

Consolidated version of the Treaty on the Functioning of the European Union. OJ C 326, pp 47–390, 26 Oct 2012

De La Rue (2019) De La Rue appointed to deliver track and trace service for all UK tobacco products. https://www.delarue.com/media-center/de-la-rue-appointed-to-deliver-track-and-trace-service-for-all-uk-tobacco-products. Accessed 24 Feb 2020

Directive 2001/37/EC of the European Parliament and of the Council of 5 June 2001 on the approximation of the laws, regulations and administrative provisions of the Member States concerning the manufacture, presentation and sale of tobacco products. OJ L 194, p 26, 18 Jul 2001

Directive 2014/40/EU of the European Parliament and of the Council of 3 April 2014 on the approximation of the laws, regulations and administrative provisions of the Member States concerning the manufacture, presentation and sale of tobacco and related products and repealing Directive 2001/37/EC. OJ L 127, pp 1–38, 29 Apr 2014

European Commission (2017) Impact Assessment Accompanying the Document Commission Implementing Regulation (EU) …/… on technical standards for the establishment and operation of a traceability system for tobacco products and Commission Implementing Decision on technical standards for security features applied to tobacco products. Commission Staff Working Document, 15 Dec 2017 SWD(2017) 455 final. https://ec.europa.eu/health/tobacco/tracking_tracing_system_en (see 'Impact Assessment'). Accessed 24 Feb 2020

European Commission (2017) Impact Assessment on Implementing Regulation on traceability system and security features for tobacco products

European Commission (2018) Annex to the Communication from the Commission to the European Parliament, the Council and the European Economic and Social Committee 2nd Action Plan to fight the illicit tobacco trade 2018–2022. European Commission, COM (2018) 846 final, 7 Dec 2018

European Commission (2018) Communication from the Commission to the European Parliament, the Council and the European Economic and Social Committee, 2nd Action Plan to fight the illicit tobacco trade 2018–2022. Brussels, 7 Dec 2018, COM (2018) 846 final. https://eur-lex.europa.eu/legal-content/EN/TXT/HTML/?uri=CELEX:52018DC0846&from=en. Accessed 24 Feb 2020

HM Government (2018) Explanatory Memorandum on the Protocol to Eliminate Illicit Trade in Tobacco Products. Her Majesty's Government. https://assets.publishing.service.gov.uk/government/uploads/system/uploads/attachment_data/file/704635/EM_Misc5.2018_Prot_Tob.pdf. Accessed 24 Feb 2020

HM Government (2018) UK ratifies global treaty to tackle illegal tobacco trade. Her Majesty's Government, 29 June 2018. https://www.gov.uk/government/news/uk-ratifies-global-treaty-to-tackle-illegal-tobacco-trade. Accessed 24 Feb 2020

HM Revenue and Customs (2013) Explanatory Memorandum on European Union Documents. 12605/13, COM (2013) 538. Her Majesty's Revenue and Customs, July 2013. http://webcache.googleusercontent.com/search?q=cache:fhV-0wp56sAJ:europeanmemoranda.cabinetoffice.gov.uk/files/2014/04/12605-13.doc+&cd=1&hl=en&ct=clnk&gl=ch. Accessed 27 Feb 2020

HMRC and UK Border Force (2015) Tackling illicit tobacco: From leaf to light The HMRC and Border Force strategy to tackle tobacco smuggling. Government of the United Kingdom. https://assets.publishing.service.gov.uk/government/uploads/system/uploads/attachment_data/file/418732/Tackling_illicit_tobacco_-_From_leaf_to_light__2015_.pdf. Accessed 24 Feb 2020

References

Protocol to Eliminate Illicit Trade in Tobacco Products. Adopted by the Conference of the Parties to the WHO FCTC, 2012. https://www.who.int/fctc/protocol/illicit_trade/protocol-publication/en/. Accessed 24 Feb 2020

The "Declaration of Competences" has been prepared pursuant to ITP Article 44 (Ratification, acceptance, approval, formal confirmation or accession). https://treaties.un.org/Pages/ViewDetails.aspx?src=TREATY&mtdsg_no=IX-4-a&chapter=9&clang=_en

The Tobacco Products (Traceability and Security Features) Regulations 2019. United Kingdom Parliament. http://www.legislation.gov.uk/uksi/2019/594/made. Accessed 24 Feb 2020

TED (2019) United Kingdom-Salford: Software package and information systems, Contract award notice, 2019/S 042-096012. Tenders Electronically Daily, OJEU. https://ted.europa.eu/TED/notice/udl?uri=TED:NOTICE:96012-2019:TEXT:EN:HTML. Accessed 24 Feb 2020

TJI (2019) Track and Trace system to be suspended in no-deal Brexit. Tobacco Journal International, 6 Sept 2019. http://www.tobaccojournal.com/Track_and_Trace_system_to_be_suspended_in_no-deal_Brexit.55449.0.html. Accessed 24 Feb 2020

Walker G (2019) UK to suspend tobacco Track and Trace system in no-deal Brexit. Convenience Store, 4 Sept 2019. https://www.conveniencestore.co.uk/news/uk-to-suspend-tobacco-track-and-trace-system-in-no-deal-brexit/597241.article. Accessed 24 Feb 2020

WHO Framework Convention on Tobacco Control—FCTC Rules of Procedure of the Meeting of the Parties. https://www.who.int/fctc/protocol/mop-rules-procedure/en/. Accessed 24 Feb 2020

WHO Framework Convention on Tobacco Control (FCTC). World Health Organization, adopted 21 May 2003 and entered into force on 27 Feb 2004. https://www.who.int/fctc/cop/about/en/. Accessed 24 Feb 2020

Open Access This chapter is licensed under the terms of the Creative Commons Attribution 4.0 International License (http://creativecommons.org/licenses/by/4.0/), which permits use, sharing, adaptation, distribution and reproduction in any medium or format, as long as you give appropriate credit to the original author(s) and the source, provide a link to the Creative Commons license and indicate if changes were made.

The images or other third party material in this chapter are included in the chapter's Creative Commons license, unless indicated otherwise in a credit line to the material. If material is not included in the chapter's Creative Commons license and your intended use is not permitted by statutory regulation or exceeds the permitted use, you will need to obtain permission directly from the copyright holder.

Chapter 7
Conclusions and Recommendations

Brexit represents an unprecedented moment for the European integration project. Despite the evident difficulties in assessing the impact of the still ongoing process on the cladenstine activity of illicit tradde, all in all, the potential effects of Brexit on illicit tobacco trade in the UK could be rather modest. One thing which emerges with certain clarity is that just as in many other policy areas, the control of the illicit trade of tobacco by the UK will depend ultemately on the Brexit scenario negotiated with EU. In the event of a leaving the single market, while losing economically on many ends, the UK would retain higher policy flexibilites. While still bound by the ITP, this may mean greater speed and flexibility in learning and improving upon existing global or regional norms in this field to its own benefit.

The data presented in this study shows that the UK is a target country for illicit tobacco trade. The country has no significant domestic production (licit or illicit), and is not a transit country for illicit products *en route* to other EU Member States. The focus is therefore mainly on how Brexit may impact illicit trade into the UK. The case of Gibraltar, where illicit products tend to move from the UK territory into (the EU) Spain, represents an exception. Gibraltar already currently enjoys a special status and maintains a rather 'hard' border with neighbouring Spain. The *2019 Withdrawal Agreement* foresees a Protocol accompanied by a bilateral *'Memorandum of Understanding on Tobacco and other Products'* with Spain, capping the price difference between adjacent territories and fostering cooperation and enforcement. This should limit the risks of an increase of illicit activities related to tobacco targeting the EU market from Gibraltar as a result of Brexit.

More generally, opportunities for smuggling into the UK may arise from an unorderly implementation of its withdrawal from the EU, a scenario that could materialize in case of 'Hard Brexit'. The acceptance of the *2019 Withdrawal Agreement* by the UK Parliament after the December 2019 elections and the start of the transition period (now set to last until the end of 2020) should prevent this. Much will of course depend on the UK's ability to implement the changes necessary for (licit) trade to be carried out in an orderly manner.

Brexit is not expected to have dramatic effects on the relevant legislation analysed. Most of it is already domestic (UK) legislation and directly applicable EU law will be retained in UK law after exit day. Whether and how in the future the UK will remain aligned to relevant EU legislation depends on several factors. The December elections brought clarity as to the most likely approach to future UK–EU relations. Now that the UK has officially withdrawn on January 31st 2020, the two parties are expected to negotiate an ambitious trade agreement.

Little, however, has been said regarding the unavoidable trade-off between ease of access to the EU markets and autonomy to diverge from EU regulation. This is particularly important for the future application of select aspects of the EU 2014 Tobacco Products Directive (TPD-2), of relevance to the control of tobacco trade. In general however, the past record and the current HMRC and UK Border Force joint national strategy in place ('*Tackling illicit tobacco: From leaf to light*') suggests that the country will maintain its strict tobacco regulations.

Two additional aspects that may have an indirect impact on illicit trade also depend on the final form of Brexit. These are import tariffs and thresholds for personal allowances for tobacco products. In an environment of elevated prices (currently among the highest in the world), the adoption of excessively (trade or fiscal) restrictive measures on tobacco may indirectly strengthen the demand for illicit products. The option of levying import tariffs on tobacco products originating from the EU would only be available in case of '*Hard Brexit*'. Thus, the materialisation of this scenario would grant the UK independent decision-making powers to establish its desired level of import duties. The complex economic constelation created by Brexit (and pegorated by the Covid-19 crisis) may push the UK into raising its import duties or internal taxes on tobacco. Under the three other Brexit scenarios, including the case of conclusion of a trade agreement, the parties would exchange tobacco products without applying import duties. If the UK remains part of the single market, it would have to abide by the EU minimum excise requirements (in this scenario the UK is till free to raise its excise given the concern of the EU legislation with minimum levels). Under all scenarios analysed, the UK would have the latitude to adopt the tobacco personal allowances threshold it wishes, without consideration for EU imposed minimum levels.

The analysis above also suggests that cooperation with EU institutions, agencies, and bodies in the areas of investigation and enforcement, as well as with the EU Member States, is an aspect that deserves specific consideration. This is of outmost importance since the UK is a target country for illicit tobacco—and a particularly attractive one because of the high price for licit products. Brexit will impact the current format of active participation in the work of the different agencies that operate to tackle illicit tobacco trade in the EU. Today, the UK takes part in EU police and judicial cooperation in criminal matters, including in the context of information exchange databases and systems, such as OLAF, Europol, Frontex and Eurojust. Cooperation has led to tangible results. Preserving the highest possible degree of interaction after Brexit is in the interest of both sides. The texts negotiated between the parties (the *2019 Withdrawal Agreement* and the non-binding *2019 Political Declaration*) only contain limited references to this important aspect. The institutions, agencies, and EU bodies considered, all provide for partnership mechanisms for non-EU members which, while not comparable to full membership, may offer a viable solution.

7 Conclusions and Recommendations

Cooperation in the fight against illicit trade in tobacco products should also be fostered at the national level, with the aim of developing a comprehensive UK national anti-illicit trade strategy covering other areas than tobacco.

Finally, illicit trade in tobacco products is a global problem and addressing it requires global solutions. There is currently considerable confusion as to the post-Brexit fate of the recently introduced track and trace system mandated by TPD-2. Its efficacy is questionable, considering the current patterns of illicit trade in tobacco products, according to which most of what is consumed in the UK originates outside of the EU (where governmentally owned track and trace systems does not exist—at least for the moment). As a party in its own right to the ITP, the UK would stand to gain from the broadest possible participation in such international initiatives.

Open Access This chapter is licensed under the terms of the Creative Commons Attribution 4.0 International License (http://creativecommons.org/licenses/by/4.0/), which permits use, sharing, adaptation, distribution and reproduction in any medium or format, as long as you give appropriate credit to the original author(s) and the source, provide a link to the Creative Commons license and indicate if changes were made.

The images or other third party material in this chapter are included in the chapter's Creative Commons license, unless indicated otherwise in a credit line to the material. If material is not included in the chapter's Creative Commons license and your intended use is not permitted by statutory regulation or exceeds the permitted use, you will need to obtain permission directly from the copyright holder.